T0320399

The Art of Investigation

The Art of Investigation examines the qualities required to be a professional, thorough, and effective investigator. As the title suggests, it delves into more than the steps and procedures involved in managing an investigation, but the "soft" skills necessary to effectively direct and intuit along the way. The editors, and contributing authors, are the best in their field and bring a wealth of real-world knowledge and experience to the subject. There are several publications available on the nuts-and-bolts of the process and stages of an investigation. That ground has been covered. However, little has been published on the investigative skills required, the traits necessary, and the qualities endemic to an inquisitive mind that can be cultivated to improve an investigator's professional skill-set.

Each chapter discusses the applicability of the traits, and requirements to the contributor's own work and experience as an investigator. In doing so, the contributors provide a story—or set of stories—from their personal experience, which demonstrates their use or a given trait and its importance in the course of their investigative work and career. This will be first-hand experience that will serve to help any investigative profession in the course of their work. The case examples included throughout are sometimes surprising, but always engaging and insightful. An investigator must keep an open mind above all else and this book will seek to "lift the veil" on the inner workings of an investigation in addition to the thought processes and inner monologues of an investigator as part of that process.

The Art of Investigation will be a welcome addition to any investigator's toolkit and will also be of interest to students in criminal justice, security and Homeland Security programs, security consultants, corporate and private security professionals, and the legal community.

The Art of Investigation

Edited by
Chelsea A. Binns
Bruce Sackman

CRC Press
Taylor & Francis Group
Boca Raton London New York

CRC Press is an imprint of the
Taylor & Francis Group, an **informa** business

CRC Press
Taylor & Francis Group
6000 Broken Sound Parkway NW, Suite 300
Boca Raton, FL 33487–2742

© 2020 by Taylor & Francis Group, LLC

CRC Press is an imprint of Taylor & Francis Group, an Informa business

No claim to original U.S. Government works

International Standard Book Number-13: 978-1-138-35378-7 (Hardback)

Visit the Taylor & Francis Web site at
www.taylorandfrancis.com

and the CRC Press Web site at
www.crcpress.com

Chelsea A. Binns
"This book is for Samantha, who was with me on this project from the very beginning."

Bruce Sackman
"To Eileen, Allison, Jonathan, and my grandchildren, Brianna and Taylor, who fill me with joy whenever they are near."

Contents

Foreword

Oscar Wilde wrote, "The truth is rarely pure and never simple." The investigative paths that the authors of the chapters in this book will take us on are often through the dark corners of our society, while others are part of the fabric of everyday life. In these unsettling places, where investigators find themselves delving into human weakness, craven indifference, and, thankfully, the rare occurrence of true evil, truth is a winding and sometimes dangerous path to justice. It is fraught with human error, inexplicable negligence and deceit. Those that seek the truth have both innate and acquired skill-sets necessary for that adventure. The innate qualities needed for the journey into truth finding are explained in this book. Without possession of these 15 attributes it would be impossible to sustain a career as an investigator. These innate gifts must be paired with acquired skills in an ever-changing world. Technology can expedite a case and experience adds to one's abilities.

This book is an adventure for those who enjoy the art of the investigation, enjoy the finesse, the strategies, incredible flexibility, and the professionalism readily apparent to those of us that ply this trade. As a career investigator into all types of criminal behavior I have investigated both wealthy and poor, and all in between. I find myself most comfortable with fellow investigators, truth seekers. The obvious is sometimes deceiving, healthy skepticism illuminates that trap. The requisite fortitude mandatory for long-term casework is fueled by the 15 themes displayed within these pages. The authors of the chapters within are heroic figures who detail their cases with these virtues and, most importantly, humanity.

In my tenure as NYPD Chief of Detectives, I have dedicated my professional life to finding the truth. I have led great men and women in that task; assembling, training and supervising roughly 6000 investigators towards that singular purpose. In many instances during a 35-year career, I interviewed many officers with the aim of seeking those with the innate abilities required for such difficult casework. Team building and networking are essential to the vagaries of human behavior and thinking, new technologies and tracking information. No one person solves an intricate and complex case. Sources of information are imperative to the mission, building one's network to solve the everyday obstacles within the case cannot be understated. I think of the Etan Patz investigation, 35 years to justice, the Baby

Hope case, 22 years to a successful prosecution—the dogged pursuit of truth and the justice it brings. Always believe that you as the investigator will solve the case, bring the investigation to a successful conclusion, and, ultimately, find the truth.

Robert Boyce,
NYPD Chief of Detectives, ret.

Acknowledgments

The authors would like to thank their contributors, who took time from their busy lives to reflect upon, research, and reveal their amazing stories and years of accumulated knowledge to our readers.

About the Editors

Chelsea A. Binns is an Assistant Professor and the Director of the Center for Safety and Private Security in the Department of Security, Fire and Emergency Management at John Jay College of Criminal Justice in New York City. She is the author of *Fraud Hotlines: Design, Performance & Assessment* published by Taylor & Francis/CRC Press. She is a licensed Private Investigator and Certified Fraud Examiner, and is the president of the New York Chapter of the Association of Certified Fraud Examiners. She is the recipient of several teaching and employee recognition awards. Her research interests are focused on corporate security matters, including background checks, corporate crime, cybercrime, investigations, and organizational fraud. She has extensive corporate security, management, and investigative experience, having worked for prestigious organizations such as Citibank, Morgan Stanley, New York City's Department of Investigation (DOI), and the New York State Office of the Attorney General. Before joining John Jay College, she was a Senior Vice President in Citibank's Fraud Surveillance Unit in New York City. Ms. Binns frequently lectures before elite audiences, including major industry groups, governmental organizations, and investigative teams. Ms. Binns has a doctorate and two master's degrees in Criminal Justice from the CUNY Graduate Center/John Jay College of Criminal Justice.

Bruce Sackman served as the Special Agent in Charge, U.S. Department of Veteran Affairs (VA), Office of Inspector General, Criminal Investigations Division, Northeast Field Office until May 2005 when he retired after 32 years' service. In this capacity, he was responsible for all major criminal investigations involving VA from West Virginia to Maine. During his tenure he was involved in hundreds of investigations involving allegations of fraud, corruption, false claims, thefts, patient assaults, pharmaceutical drug diversions, and suspicious hospital deaths. He was also responsible for supervising the successful investigation of the nation's first homicide conviction in connection with pharmaceutical research. His cases involving medical professionals who have murdered their patients have been featured on the Discovery Health Channel, CNN, MSNBC, *America's Most Wanted*, and on Home Box Office. He is the recipient of many awards for his investigations and for his efforts in encouraging the profession of forensic nursing. Mr. Sackman has lectured at several forensic-related conferences, State police organizations, the Federal Law Enforcement Training Center, universities, and medical-related symposia.

He is the co-author of the new book *Behind the Murder Curtain, Special Agent Bruce Sackman Hunts Doctors and Nurses Who Kill Our Veterans* and the article "When the ICU becomes a Crime Scene," published by *Critical Care Nursing Quarterly.*

Mr. Sackman is currently self-employed as a licensed private investigator in New York City, specializing in healthcare-related matters. Under contract, he directs major investigations for a large New York metropolitan regional healthcare system.

Contributors

Gil Alba is a nationally known private investigator and security consultant, having formed Alba Investigations Inc. in 1998. He was the President of the Associated Licensed Detectives of New York State and also received the honor of being named their "Investigator of the Year" in 2004. Mr. Alba had a distinguished career with the New York City Police Department, attaining the highest investigative rank, First Grade Detective, and worked with the Major Case Squad and the FBI/NYPD Violent Crime Task Force specializing in difficult and unusual cases. Mr. Alba is a frequent guest on Fox News, CNN, MSNBC, BBC, World News, and other news networks for his expertise when disasters occur, such as school shootings, mass shootings, missing persons, and terrorist acts. A one-hour documentary about Mr. Alba's missing persons murder cases has been featured on MSNBC and *48 Hours*. Mr. Alba is a frequent keynote and guest speaker at high schools, colleges, universities, and business functions. He facilitated the rescue of Harvey Weinstein's high-profile kidnapping case, leading to the return of a $3 million ransom. The New York City Police Department's Major Case Squad, working together with other units comprising the best investigators in the world, saved a life in this high profile investigation. Alba Investigations Inc. is licensed by the New York State Department of State, Division of Licensing Services, bonded and insured. Mr. Alba holds a BA Degree in Behavioral Science from Concordia College in Bronxville, NY; he received an Associate's Degree in Metallurgy from Erie County Tech, and attended John Jay College of Criminal Justice, and served in the Army Reserves.

Daniel R. Alonso—as a prosecutor, corporate defense lawyer, and compliance and investigations consultant—has specialized in financial crime, corruption, and ethics. He served as an Assistant U.S. Attorney and Chief of the Criminal Division in the U.S. Attorney's Office for the Eastern District of New York, and has also served as the Chief Assistant District Attorney in the Manhattan District Attorney's Office. As a lawyer in private practice at the law firm of Kaye Scholer LLP (now Arnold & Porter Kaye Scholer LLP), Mr. Alonso represented corporations and corporate executives in internal investigations and white-collar and enforcement matters, and served as the federal-court-appointed receiver of IATrading.com, as discussed in the text. Since 2014, he has been Managing Director and General Counsel of Exiger, a global compliance and investigations firm specializing in technology-based compliance and investigative solutions. Mr. Alonso was formerly the Co-Chair of the New York State White Collar Crime Task Force, and the Chair of the Council on Criminal Justice of the New York City Bar Association, as well as a gubernatorial appointee to the New York State Commission on Public Integrity. Currently, he is a member of the New York State Attorney Grievance Committee and the New York State Bar Association's Committee on Standards of Attorney Conduct, and is also on the Board of Editors of the *Journal of Financial Crime.*

Kim Anklin is a Principal/Partner and Legal Strategist for Management Resources Ltd. of New York. She is a former Crime and Intelligence Analyst from the City of Ventura, CA. Kim brings her 20 years of experience, analytical skills, and innovative solutions to every investigation and special project. Her areas of expertise include working in partnership with attorneys, providing investigative strategic analysis for complex civil and criminal cases, as well as working with clients and their families to help them navigate through their legal battles. Kim holds a Bachelor of Science Degree in Psychology and a Master's Degree in Public Administration from California Lutheran University. Kim has worked with Bob Rahn for 16 years. During this time, they have conducted thousands of investigations, with cases involving insurance fraud, wrongful death, civil rights violations, criminal defense, and missing persons. One notable investigation Kim and Bob conducted was the case of missing person Vernon Kent Jones, which was featured on CBS News.

James A. Gagliano, a 1987 graduate of the United States Military Academy and former U.S. Army Officer, served in the FBI for a quarter-century until retiring as a Supervisory Special Agent in December of 2015. While in the FBI, he served in a variety of investigative, SWAT, undercover, and leadership positions, domestically and overseas. He received a M.P.S. in Homeland Security, Criminal Justice Leadership from St. John's University in 2017, where he currently teaches undergraduates and is pursuing a doctorate in Homeland Security. He also appears on CNN as one of the network's full-time law enforcement analysts, and lectures on leadership topics for corporate clients and in university settings.

Charles-Eric Gordon is an investigative attorney with an office in Woodbury, New York, where his practice principally involves locating people who have been absent for a long period of time and/or about whom little information is known. He has been interviewed by the *New York Times*, the *New York Law Journal*, the *Wall Street Journal*, the *New York Post*, *Newsday*, and *Crains New York Business*, and has been seen on television in both the United States and Australia. Charles-Eric obtained his Juris Doctor from Brooklyn Law School in 1979 and has been admitted to the New York State Bar and the Federal District Courts for the Southern and Eastern Districts of New York. A former City of New York administrative law judge and Special Investigator, he serves on the Board of Directors of the Society of

Professional Investigators and is a member of the World Association of Detectives, the American Academy for Professional Law Enforcement, the National Law Enforcement Associates, and the Associated Licensed Detectives of New York State.

Gareth Howie's background in the field of investigation originated upon leaving high school when he enlisted with the Royal Air Force to serve as a military police officer. He then went on to be a constable within the Metropolitan Police in North London. Upon returning to the North East of England, Gareth has worked as an investigator in both the banking and civil service sectors; investigating such matters as fraud, complaints, and staff misconduct. Over the last four to five years he freelanced in the private investigation sector within the region but became very disillusioned with the lack of professionalism, questionable ethics, etc., that he was encountering. In 2016 he set up Surmount Investigations as the counterpoint to this representation in the field in his area—Surmount being a professional problem-solving investigatory and surveillance service for individuals and businesses, driven by a high ethical standard and integrity-driven approach to lawful and legitimate evidence gathering. Through Surmount, Gareth specializes in criminal defense/ litigation support for law firms throughout the North East of England and assisting in investigations and surveillance operations for businesses and organizations pertaining to employee conduct concerns.

Bill Jorgenson is a former associate commissioner at the New York City Department of Investigation (DOI). At DOI he was in charge of Training, Outreach, Background Investigations, Investigative Audits, and several other related units. Prior to this assignment, Bill supervised three divisions within DOI which investigated cases involving fraud and misconduct in New York City school construction, New York City public housing, city elected officials, and non-profit recipients of city grant money. Before joining DOI in the summer of 2014, Bill's career as a prosecutor spanned three decades in various offices throughout the New York metropolitan area. Bill worked as an assistant district attorney in the Staten Island District Attorney's Office and the Office of the Special Narcotics Prosecutor in Manhattan, where he handled numerous trials involving narcotics and homicide cases. Bill then worked in the New York State Attorney General's office where he investigated and prosecuted complex auto insurance fraud conspiracies. Bill rounded out his time as an assistant district attorney conducting white collar prosecutions in the Nassau County District Attorney's Office. He focused on the investigation and prosecution of financial crimes and public corruption.

Bill Majeski is the President of Majeski Associates Inc., an investigative firm in operation since 1988, creating solutions and serving a broad spectrum of clients. He is also a Senior Advisor for Hetherington Group. Mr. Majeski is a veteran of the New York City Police Department where he had a distinguished career for 21 years as a Detective and earned a reputation for being sagacious. His law enforcement expertise encompasses a vast array of criminal and internal investigations, from homicides through to political corruption. He has completed numerous complex civil litigations as well as criminal matters. He developed the "Power Interview", and provides lectures and training in communication skills, interviewing, corporate litigation, and other topics. Mr. Majeski has a BS Degree from John Jay College of Criminal Justice and is a graduate of the FBI National Academy, Quantico, Virginia. He is a practicing polygraph examiner and has personally conducted thousands of interviews, interrogations, and polygraph examinations. He is a former Adjunct Instructor in the Graduate Criminal Justice Program of Long Island University, Centenary University and Essex County College. For ten years he directed academic programs as the Chief Instructor for the New York Institute of Polygraph Science. Bill has over 200 appearances on various news networks, has been featured in the *NY Times, Parade Magazine*, and the *NY Daily News*, has authored the *Lie Detection Book* (Ballantine Publications), and has contributed to many other publications.

Tom Martin is a retired 22-year veteran of the New York State Police. He served the majority of his career as the supervisor of a full-time, full-service forensic crime scene response unit, investigating the forensic aspects of major and violent crimes. Tom has extensive forensic experience and expertise in various forensic disciplines, including bloodstain pattern analysis, shooting reconstruction, and latent print identification. He continues to work regularly in the field of forensic reconstructions as the owner of a private consulting and training company.

Cynthia Navarro has been in private investigations for almost 40 years. Her specialties are intellectual property, licensing, corporate investigations, open source intelligence, cyber investigation, online investigations, fraud, business due diligence, and business intelligence. She has trained law enforcement and corporate investigators in Asia, Europe, and throughout the United States. Cynthia currently oversees forensics, cybersecurity, dark web and open source intelligence cases.

Susan Pickman has managed and conducted civil, criminal, and regulatory investigations for over 30 years. She has experience in due diligence, fraud detection and prevention, and management audits. She has also been a "street cop," had fiduciary responsibility for 40 million dollars, and managed an internal affairs unit. She is the Faculty Advisor for the John Jay College Auxiliary University Program (AUP) Detachment and USCG Auxiliary Assistant District Staff Officer for Incident Management.

Bob Rahn is the President of Management Resources Ltd. of New York, which he founded in 1994. He is a former homicide detective with over 40 years of investigative experience. Bob holds a Bachelor's Degree in Sociology from St. Francis College and a Master's Degree in Public Administration from John Jay College of Criminal Justice. He has taught as a General Topics Instructor at the Orange

County Police Academy and as an Adjunct Instructor of Criminal Justice, at Mount Saint Mary College. Bob is a member of the Lieutenant's Benevolent Association of the New York City Police Department and the Emerald Society of the NYPD. Bob has worked with Kim Anklin for 16 years. During this time, they have conducted thousands of investigations, with cases involving insurance fraud, wrongful death, civil rights violations, criminal defense, and missing persons. One notable investigation Bob and Kim conducted was the case of missing person Vernon Kent Jones, which was featured on CBS News.

Matthew Spaier is a Licensed and Bonded Private Investigator in New York State. He is the owner of Satellite Investigations and is the Second Vice President of the Associated Licensed Detectives of New York State (ALDONYS). He is also a member of the Society of Professional Investigators (SPI), The New York City Chapter of Certified Fraud Examiners and the World Association of Detectives (WAD). He is a Partner for Justice with the New York State Trial Lawyers Association. Matthew is a graduate of CUNY John Jay College of Criminal Justice and has lectured at the college about geo-tagging and geo-fencing technology. He has also lectured about this topic to various state private investigator associations.

Emmanuelle Welch, a Licensed Private Investigator and Certified Fraud Examiner, owns French Connection Research, a private investigative agency in New York State and Washington, DC. Founded in 2004 as a research business out of Los Angeles, the agency has branched out into white collar crime investigations, international asset searches, opposition research, and cross-Atlantic fraud cases, quite often involving French individuals living with a certain panache (and ill-gotten money) under Instagram-worthy Florida skies. She serves as the vice-president of New York's Society for Professional Investigators (SPI).

Machiko Yamamoto, CFE, CPCI, earned an undergraduate degree in Japan and upon moving to the United States, received certifications in Crime and Intelligence Analysis and Crime Scene Investigation, and earned a Master's degree in Criminal Justice. During this time, Machiko worked as a volunteer at the Support Network for Battered Women and the Riverside County Sheriff's Department Crime Analysis Unit. Upon her return to Japan, she worked as an assistant professor in a research and teaching position. She worked for several years at a risk consulting company as a Security/Criminal Investigator and is currently a security manager at a leading global travel security assistance firm. She is a certified fraud examiner (CFE) and a Certified Professional Criminal Investigator (CPCI). As a CFE, she has been very involved with the Association of Certified Fraud Examiners (ACFE) Japan chapter, conducting seminars and creating original content for their newsletter.

Introduction— Editors' Note

Within these pages are over 500 years of imagination, skill, and technique provided to educate, inform, and even entertain students of investigation. Whether you are a criminal justice major, a true crime reader, or anyone involved in the investigative process, this book will serve to enlighten you on the experiences and lessons learned by some of the most seasoned professionals around.

Containing the knowledge of 17 investigative professionals, we believe this to be the first book to provide this level of guidance, experience, and wisdom to the student of investigations. Whether your work is criminal, civil, or administrative, upon completion of this book you will be markedly better prepared to begin your journey to uncover the facts.

This book was borne out of our collective experience as investigators, academics, industry group leaders, public speakers, and authors.

Investigators are the most amazing people. They possess the most incredible combination of skills, including: adaptability, confidence, creativity, curiosity, discretion, empathy, energy, ingenuity, initiative, integrity, patience, professionalism, self-control, skepticism, and tenacity.

As you will see in *The Art of Investigation*, their work is truly an art to be emulated. With this text, it is possible to obtain a rare insight into the work of the investigator in numerous industries.

As investigators ourselves, we have worked with many investigative professionals over our careers. And we noticed that the ones who possessed the skills covered in this book were among the most successful.

By carefully selecting key words to define each chapter, we inform the reader of the expertise essential to mastering this art. To support our selection we provide an amazing case study and detailed instruction to help train the reader on techniques that will assist their own investigative efforts.

Chapter 1

Tenacity

Kim Anklin and Bob Rahn

Tenacity is a quality that all investigators must have in order to be successful. Tenacity in an investigator gives you the ability to work a case until all leads are exhausted and then go back and look at it again to figure out what you missed, to start from scratch and re-do every step of the investigation again. To some, this may sound tedious, but this skill is critical in investigations and separates the good investigators from the great ones. Tenacity is the ability not to take anything for granted, to examine every bit of evidence you have no matter how small and insignificant, and to keep going when you think you don't have anywhere else to go. It means never giving up, like a dog chasing a ball. Yes, you will get discouraged. However, when you are rewarded with a great outcome in a case, you will soon realize the benefit.

Tenacity comes to people in different ways. Take the authors of this chapter, for instance. For Bob, it was learned over the years. Bob honed his tenacity while investigating hundreds of homicides during the 1980s in Brooklyn, while working with some of the most highly experienced and talented detectives in the world. For other investigators, such as Kim, tenacity is a trait they are born with. Kim is extremely persistent by nature. She is very committed to her casework, and remains engaged until she gets the answers to her questions. Her experience as an analyst studying and reviewing data and fact patterns makes her an outstanding investigator.

Case Study in Tenacity

We started conducting criminal defense investigations in 2008 after attending an Investigators' Conference in Worcester, Massachusetts. The keynote speaker at this conference was renowned defense attorney F. Lee Bailey. During his speech, he said prosecutors not only had awesome power and authority, but also had unlimited resources to prosecute individuals. They had the full resources of the police department and the prosecutor's office. This was a tremendous disadvantage for the defense who had none of these resources at their disposal. Mr. Bailey said this dynamic meant the scales of justice were tipped against the defense, meaning prosecutors had a distinct advantage. His statements inspired us to specialize in criminal defense investigations. We decided to do so on a case-by-case basis, so that we could be more selective in the investigations we conducted. After conducting a few pre-trial defense investigations, we found that we enjoyed working on them, and were good at it. The rest, as they say, is history.

It wasn't until the spring of 2012 that we entered the world of post-trial convictions. More specifically, wrongful convictions. In that year, we worked on a case that really demonstrates our tenacity. In 2012 we received a telephone call from a family member of a man named Jonathan Fleming. In August 1989, Jonathan Fleming was arrested for killing Daryll Rush, aka Black near a Brooklyn housing project. At trial, the jury heard evidence that Fleming was at Disney World with family members at the time of the murder, but he was nevertheless convicted of homicide and sentenced to 25 years to life in prison. The family was looking for an investigator to help them prove that Fleming was wrongfully convicted. At the time, the family said they didn't have the funds available to hire us.

We did not hear from them again until 2013. We were told that they now had the resources to hire us but were a bit hesitant about engaging another investigator. We learned that, prior to us, the family had hired four different private investigators and were dismayed about hiring another one because those PIs had been unable to help them. The family interviewed us over the phone and Jonathan Fleming interviewed us extensively from his prison cell. After answering all of their questions they decided to hire us. We had an agreement that we would never take a case unless we discussed it and both agreed on accepting it. One of us, Bob, made the initial decision to take the case and now had the daunting task of convincing the other, Kim. Bob knew it was a new and unknown challenge for them. He called Kim and said, "Hey listen remember that call we had in 2012 about the wrongful conviction investigation?" Well they called back and want to hire us, so I took the case". After a brief pause, Kim said "Okay" and so we, Bob and Kim, were in the wrongful conviction business.

As wrongful conviction investigators, we learned that tenacity is a mandatory skill-set in this business. In the majority of wrongful conviction cases, the client or the incarcerated individual has been convicted for 10, 15, 20, or 25 years to life. In Fleming's case he was serving 25 to life. When you are investigating cases like these you are up against two major obstacles. The first being that it involves a wrongful conviction, which is a challenge by nature. In these cases, the outcome had already been decided in a court of law and is very challenging to reverse. The second obstacle is that so much time has passed since the conviction, until the time an investigator gets involved, that it is also now a "cold case." By definition, a cold case is one where all the leads have been exhausted.[1] Key witnesses in the case may have moved away and or died. Documents may have been lost or destroyed. There are often a host of obstacles and you don't know what you are facing until you begin reviewing the case files.

On a sunny Sunday morning in April 2013, we commenced the Wrongful Conviction Investigation of Jonathan Fleming. We drove to Queens and met with Jonathan's former attorney who had been handling his case pro-bono for several years. The attorney handed us a large box of police reports and transcripts and said, "I have done all I could. Good luck."

We began with the three-step protocol for investigating wrongful convictions. This protocol was developed by Private Investigator Susan Carlson.[2] Susan has since passed away, but her written works continue to inspire professional investigators. Step one of her protocol is Preparation. This involves an extensive review of the documents. You must familiarize yourself with the entire case and know it just as well as the client does. This must be done prior to any interviews or field investigations. Investigators must be able to determine whether the witnesses are telling the truth during future interviews. The second step is Inquiry. This involves the field work. Visiting the crime scene, tracking down all known witnesses and attempting to get statements. You also want to look for potential unknown witnesses. That is, people who know something about the case, but never came forward and/or were never spoken to by the police or prosecutor. The final step is Documentation, which involves preparing your report so it can be presented to the prosecutor or the court.

The preparation phase for us involved pouring through the box of documents that Jonathan's former lawyer gave us. Kim methodically read literally thousands of pages of pre-trial hearings, trial transcripts, post-trial hearings, as well as writs and motions which were submitted over the years. Here, tenacity was critical. Bob reviewed the police reports initially to determine their validity and accuracy, then Kim reviewed them again. Kim then conducted an analysis of all the documents to determine what we had and what was missing. During this time, we had numerous telephone conversations with Jonathan from his prison cell. We asked him questions and picked his brain about the case. The preparation process took almost a month, but when we had finished, we were both confident we knew the case better than anyone.

We learned there was no physical evidence linking Jonathan to the murder. No fingerprints, no DNA, and no ballistics. Jonathan was convicted solely on the testimony of an eye witness, who we will call witness A, that the police had picked up in a stolen car and who was in possession of crack cocaine. It was later determined that Witness A was given a deal by the prosecutor—if she testified against Jonathan, charges against her would be dropped. Witness A agreed to the deal. However, just before she testified, she told the police and prosecutor she changed her mind, because she would be lying, and she did not want to take the stand and lie under oath. At the time, Witness A was eight months pregnant. The police and prosecutor told her that unless she testified to what was stated in the original deal she had made, they would make sure she had her baby in jail. The witness reluctantly testified, which resulted in Jonathan being convicted. After the trial, the witness told Jonathan's lawyer that she wanted to recant her testimony because she was coerced by the police and prosecutor. The lawyer petitioned the trial judge and a 330 hearing, or a post-trial hearing, was conducted in front of the same judge that presided over Jonathan's trial. Witness A told the judge she wanted to recant her testimony because it was coerced and untrue. The judge ruled that the witness had "no credibility" and believed she was lying about the coercion. The judge decided that the conviction would stand.

During the second phase of the protocol, we went into the field to make inquiries as to what happened in the case. The first thing we did was visit the crime scene. Once there we photographed the scene, examined the location where the victim was shot and retraced his steps while he was running away, and examined and photographed the location where the victim collapsed and died. We also compared the location of the shooting to the location where witness A claimed to be when she witnessed the homicide. Bob stood at the location of the shooting while Kim went to where the eye witness claimed she was.

We found some problems with the original testimony. The homicide occurred at about two in the morning. Our crime scene examination was conducted at approximately ten in the morning in broad daylight. Once in place, Bob attempted to photograph Kim's location, but could not see her. He called her on the phone and told her to wave her arms. He still could not see her. It wasn't until he used a pair of binoculars that could he finally see where Kim was. They then measured the distance from where the shooting occurred to where the eyewitness stated she was. It turned out the eyewitness was 421 feet away from the location of the shooting. Again, the shooting took place at 2 am. The witness testified at trial that she was smoking crack most of the day and was not wearing her glasses, which she needs for distance. Yet, she testified that she could see Jonathan's face as he shot the victim.

Let me put this into perspective. If anyone has ever been to Yankee Stadium, imagine standing at home plate and looking out into the center field seats, which are approximately 420 feet away, then imagine being able to pick out the face of someone sitting in one of those seats. This simple exercise of visiting, photographing and measuring the crime scene told us there was something very wrong with this case.

We also found issues with another witness's statement to police. Another witness interviewed by the police, but who never got called to testify, was a women who lived in the building that directly faced the courtyard where Black was shot. We will call her CK. She knew Black and was friendly with him. CK told the police that prior to the homicide, three men came to her apartment looking for Black. She knew two of the men by name and gave a very detailed physical description of the third person to the police, who was carrying a gun in his waistband. One was Jonathan's cousin, the other was a man named Joe (whom we learned was now deceased). CK provided this information to the police, yet they never brought these men in for questioning. It was at this point of the investigation that Kim looked at Bob and said, "I think Jonathan is really innocent."

Three additional witnesses testified at Jonathan's trial, although none of them were eyewitnesses. They were prosecution witnesses who were used to try and destroy Jonathan's alibi about being in Florida, despite the fact he had plane tickets, hotel receipts, photos and a video of him and his family in Disneyworld. We located these witnesses; one was in living in Albany, NY, one in Puerto Rico and the third was in New York. We were able to interview two out of the three—the third kept running until he was eventually arrested for murder and kidnapping in Queens.

Next, we called the Kings County District Attorney's Office, Conviction Review Unit, to determine what they would need from us to reopen the case. They said to consider a case to be re-investigated, we would have to show that we found "newly discovered evidence." They informed us that a witness simply recanting their prior testimony was not sufficient.

This is when the tenacity really kicked in. We had to hit the streets again and find new evidence. Namely, people who knew something about the case, but never spoke to the police or prosecutors. It took a lot of work, but eventually, we did. We learned of a woman, "B", who had never been spoken to by the police and never testified at the trial. We tried for a month to sit down with B and get a statement from her. She finally consented and she agreed to meet Bob in a park in the Brownsville section of Brooklyn. On the day of the meeting B showed up with a male friend and met Bob, while Kim and another investigator by the name of Scott Wagner watched in a nearby car.

This meeting was very informative. B stated that on the night of the homicide, she was at her mother's house. All of a sudden Jonathan's cousin, her brother Joe, who we mentioned earlier, and another male she knew as Rose (also known as 'Lips'), came running into the house. B took her brother Joe to the side and asked him what happened. Joe told her that Rose "popped" (killed) Black (Darryl Rush). After telling Bob this story, B agreed to provide a written statement as to what she saw and heard. This statement also corroborated what CK had told the police about the three men who were in her house before the homicide. *This* was the newly discovered evidence that we needed.

Next, we set up a meeting with John O'Mara, the Chief of the Kings County DA's Conviction Review Unit to present this new evidence to him and his investigators. Based upon the statement from B, Mr. O'Mara agreed to reopen Jonathan's case and assigned it to the DA investigators. In an unprecedented move, Mr. O'Mara authorized us to work together with his investigators on the case. This was unique in that for the first time detectives from the DA's Office were working hand in hand, sharing information with Defense Investigators, all with the same goal—to determine if Jonathan Fleming was in fact wrongfully convicted.

Then we got another break in the case. Prior to working with the DA investigators we learned the whereabouts of Jonathan's cousin. He was living in a small town in

South Carolina, about an hour and a half from Myrtle Beach. We really wanted to speak with him and to try to get a statement from him in order to clear Jonathan. We discussed this new information with the DA's investigators and they all had a second meeting with Bureau Chief O'Mara. We told him we planned to go down to South Carolina to interview him. Mr. O'Mara jokingly said, "Do you really think he is going to confess to murder?" Kim looked at him and said, "If we can find him we will get him to talk to us." Mr. O'Mara laughed and then told his detectives to go with us to South Carolina.

The trip to South Carolina would further demonstrate our tenacity. In November of 2013 we arrived in South Carolina and coordinated the plan to visit Jonathan's cousin with the DA investigators and the local Sheriff's Department. We went to the cousin's house, but no one was home. The neighbor said we had just missed the cousin, who went to his aunt's house a few miles away. Once at the aunt's house, we learned that the cousin had been there, but had left about five minutes prior to our arrival. The aunt said the cousin was driving a teal colored Chrysler 200. We recalled passing a car matching that description on the way over to the aunt's house. The car was headed in the opposite direction back toward the cousin's home. Everyone jumped back into their cars and went rushing back to the cousin's house. When they arrived the cousin was observed exiting the house and getting back in his car. The Sheriff's Deputies stopped him and he was informed that investigators from New York wanted to speak with him.

Next, the lengthy interviews took place. At this point his mother and aunt showed up and they were told the purpose of the visit. Everyone went into the back yard and sat down at a picnic table under a big tree. The cousin was reluctant to talk at first and his mother did not want him to say anything. We, along with the DA investigators, took turns talking with the cousin. It was an unusually warm November day, the sun was shining and everyone at the table was sweating. The questioning went on for about four hours. We showed him multiple affidavits where witnesses had placed him at the scene of the homicide with two other people. They also placed him driving Jonathan's car that night. At this point we told the cousin "Look we didn't come all the way from New York on a hunch. All of these witnesses placed you at the scene driving the car. Tell us, are we at least headed in the right direction?" The cousin looked at his mother and his aunt, gave a big sigh and said, "Yes, you're in the right direction."

We finally got some fruitful information. The cousin said Jonathan went to Florida and Jonathan loaned him his car while he was gone. He said on the night of the shooting he picked up Joe and the third individual who we knew as "Lips." They drove to a housing project and parked the car on Humboldt Street and they all got out. The cousin said that the three individuals were in the courtyard in front of the building when he was talking to a friend of his and he saw "Lips" talking to Darrell Rush, aka Black. All of a sudden he heard a "pop" and everybody started to run. He and Joe ran back to the car, "Lips" jumped into the back seat and said "let's get out of here I just 'popped' Black." The cousin drove the car back to his mother's house and they all ran inside where they encountered Joe's sister and told her what happened."

Now, we needed to get a statement. After hearing this story, the DA investigators told the cousin they wanted to record his statement. He gave them permission, and they recorded his statement. Next, they immediately contacted their office in Brooklyn, New York and briefed Chief O'Mara. An affidavit was prepared by the District Attorney's office and faxed down to the Sheriff's Department in South Carolina. The cousin was taken over to the Sheriff's Department where we had an opportunity to review the affidavit and the cousin signed his name to it, which made the statement official. The cousin was then told that at some point he would have to come to New York and speak with the District Attorney from the Conviction Review Unit regarding his statement. He agreed to do so.

Then we got some news that could change the outcome of the case. The date was November 4, 2013, Election Day. We were elated by the way the interview turned out, and decided to celebrate with a nice dinner and discussion about our success. While at dinner, the news came on the television that the District Attorney in Brooklyn had been voted out of office and a new District Attorney had won the election. We all looked at each other and wondered how this was going to affect the outcome of the case. We couldn't wait to get back to New York.

When we arrived back in New York, it was still unclear how the election would impact the case against Jonathan Fleming, and we wouldn't find out for several more weeks. In the meantime, the Conviction Review Unit (CRU) continued their investigation into the case.

More interviews were conducted, which brought an important lead in the case. The CRU brought the cousin up from South Carolina and interviewed him again regarding his written statement. They also wanted to interview Jonathan, so they brought him down from Wende correctional institution and took him to Rikers Island. Then they brought him to the DA's for a formal interview. Immediately after Jonathan's interview, the prosecutor from CRU slid a piece of paper across the table to us and Jonathan's attorney. She said, "Here, these may be of interest to you." The document was a telephone receipt from the hotel in Orlando, Florida, showing that the phone bill in Jonathan's room had been paid a few hours before the homicide took place. This completely destroyed the original prosecutor's theory that Jonathan could have left Florida, flew to New York, committed the homicide, and gone back to Florida.

This evidence was the proverbial "smoking gun" in the case. This document was found in the original police file and in the DA's file and had never been turned over to the defense attorney at the original trial. This was a clear violation of the *Brady* v. *Maryland*, 373 U.S. 83, which was a landmark United States Supreme Court case which established that the prosecution must turn over to the defense all evidence that might exonerate the defendant.

Needless to say, we were stunned, yet excited. This was the evidence that we needed to get Jonathan exonerated. The Prosecutor said that she had a few more loose ends to tie up in their investigation and then she would submit a final report to her supervisors for their review.

We hoped that Jonathan could be released by Christmas. This unfortunately, would not be the case. The incumbent District Attorney Charles Hynes refused to act on the exoneration, instead leaving it for the new incoming District Attorney Kenneth Thompson to handle. Coincidentally Mr. Hynes was the District Attorney at the time Jonathan was convicted in 1989.

His release would take even longer than expected. Mr. Thompson would not be appointed as the new District Attorney until January of 2014. Once he was sworn in, he needed to be brought up to speed on all the cases in his office. This meant there would be additional delays in our client's release. Finally, on April 7, 2014, a year and a day after we started our investigation, Jonathan walked out of court into the arms of his elderly mother, and was a free man.

The exoneration of Jonathan Fleming has become the career-changing case for us. The news coverage spanned the globe almost instantly. At the time we took the case, Mr. Fleming had served over 23 years of his sentence (25 years to life) for a crime, he always maintained, of which he was innocent. A crime we helped to prove he did not commit.

We have received many accolades for our painstaking work to free Jonathan, including the Investigator of the Year Award from the New Jersey Licensed Private Investigator Association (NJLPIA) and the Associated License Detectives of New York State (ALDONYS). We are pleased for this recognition because it has brought awareness to the plight of the wrongfully convicted. To this end, we have spoken publicly in several media and educational platforms about the wrongfully convicted, prosecutorial misconduct and the need to educate the public. We have also been invited on numerous radio and podcast shows. We, along with Jonathan Fleming, spoke at St. Francis College, a talk that was later published on YouTube. In addition, we were guest speakers for Penn State University's MOOC (Massive Online Course), offered through Coursera, titled *Presumed Innocent? The Social Science of Wrongful Conviction*, which has over 15,000 enrolled students from across the world discussing 'how' and 'why' wrongful convictions occur.

Ultimately we credit our success to our tenacity, which was further inspired by Jonathan's mother, Patricia Fleming. She made us promise to never stop fighting for her son. We took that oath quite seriously. You will often hear Kim say,

> She was not just a mother who believed in her son's innocence, as any mother would have, she was with him in Orlando, Florida, at the time of the Brooklyn homicide. Her level of suffering was unlike anything anyone could ever imagine. Every day, we are grateful to have had the good fortune to fulfill our promise to her.

Unfortunately, Mrs. Fleming passed away about a year after Jonathan was released, but it was her contagious tenacity that inspired us to keep going.

Now, we encourage our colleagues to take these types of cases. Kim has often said publicly that this investigation was the most rewarding work she has ever done. Specifically, Kim said, "I used to lose sleep over my client, but now I lose sleep thinking: how many others are the same situation out there?"

Notes

1. National Institute of Justice, "What is a Cold Case." Available at: https://nij.gov/ journals/260/pages/what-is-cold-case.aspx.
2. "Post Conviction Relief – The Role of the Legal Investigator," *PI Magazine*, March/ April 2013.

Chapter 2

Self-control

Gil Alba

Defining Self-control

By definition, self-control is a form of restraint exercised over one's own impulses, emotions or desires.[1] Exercising self-control is a rare and powerful opportunity to make a difference in our lives. Controlling our thoughts and emotions is essential to achieving goals.

There are simple things you can do to remain in control. Maintaining self-control can keep you from feeling the negative effects of failure. Failing is a part of life that's inevitable, but managing those failures when overwhelmed requires extra positive reinforcement. Self-control studies show that exercise and being prepared makes a person feel more in control. Perhaps just preparing a simple list and organizing your work prior to a major deadline might be all you need towards attaining self-control.

You will find that exercising self-control in the workplace can save your job and further enhance your career. From my experience, when conducting a delicate investigation and trying to meet a deadline, your supervisor can sometimes cause you anxiety by making a personal remark that is irritating about your work habits. When you are under such stress, you might be tempted to respond with a facetious comment. However, you are urged to exercise self-control and hold your comments, as they may have implications at a later time. According to best-selling author Bohdi Sanders, you should "never respond to an angry person with a fiery comeback, even if he deserves it.... Don't allow his anger to become your anger."[2]

Building self-control begins with your everyday experiences and continues in your professional life. Investigators have to think on their feet and immediately react to circumstances that may be dangerous or have a profound effect on their investigation. Practicing self-control is critical to achieving success under these circumstances.

I became a police officer in 1968. The late 1960s and early 1970s were a tough time for law enforcement. New York City was considered the crime capital of the world and I was first assigned to one of the most difficult police precincts in the city, the Four One (41), aka "Fort Apache," located in the South Bronx. This was a dangerous assignment. But I had the strong feeling that people needed me there and that I could make a difference. And in retrospect, perhaps I did. During my tenure with the NYPD, the crime rate decreased nearly 90 percent, making NYC currently one of the safest cities in the world. In the late 1990s, I retired as a First Grade Detective from the NYPD, assigned to the Major Case Squad and the NYPD/FBI Violent Task Force. I formed Alba Investigations, Inc. in 1998.

Numerous times, throughout my police career, I determined that having self-control made a given situation manageable—whether I was in an extremely dangerous situation or performing a routine task as simple as preparing reports in a timely manner. Skills that improve your self-control and thus are enormously useful to new investigators are public speaking, writing and maintaining knowledge of current events.

Public speaking skills are critical for investigators. Being verbally articulate helps you to gain confidence. Public speaking skills enable you to communicate your thoughts and intentions to individuals, such as CEOs and upper management, recruiters, teachers and interviewers. As a supervisor or executive in the field of investigations, public speaking skills are necessary for conducting training lectures and briefing the public. You can become a better speaker by taking speech courses, taking acting classes, making a video and watching it critically, practicing in the mirror. You will want to have a great answer prepared for the question "tell me about yourself" as this is a question that you will be constantly asked. Having a cold, rehearsed answer to this question will serve to relax you under stressful public speaking conditions and will serve as a great ice breaker.

Writing skills are exceptionally necessary in the investigative field. You will write a lot of reports. The language used in those reports will be very important. You can enhance your writing skills by taking writing courses, practicing writing on your own by developing relevant topics in your field and writing about them, writing research papers, writing for a newspaper, and getting published.

Investigators should also have at least a basic understanding of current events. It is important to know what is going on in the world. This is essential for many reasons. Knowledge of current events will facilitate conversations with people, to include coworkers, supervisors and investigative subjects. There are many ways you can do this today. You can read the paper, watch the news—domestic, international and local—and follow politics.

In my current role, I investigate many different types of cases. However, I have gained a great deal of knowledge and expertise involving missing persons cases with unusual circumstances. Missing person cases are unique yet require all of the same fundamental investigative procedures and skills that you would use to perform virtually any type of investigation. Missing person cases may not be profitable, but volunteering and helping distraught families is simply, pure gratification. These cases touch me, due to the raw emotions involved with missing a loved one and not knowing what happened to them.

I have investigated several matters involving men and women who disappear. Often, their loved ones are frustrated because they believe law enforcement is taking too long to solve their case. Yet these cases can take a while to solve. Finding a body of an alleged murdered missing person—a murder where no weapon, no evidence, no witnesses, no body and no smoking gun exists—is improbable, but it is not impossible.

Needless to say, these cases are challenging to solve due to the complexities involved. There is often not a crime scene and evidence can be scant. Thus, the investigator must keep in mind the myriad possibilities for what may have occurred in order to find the truth. There can be many possible explanations for someone's disappearance in a missing person case. The person could be dead or alive. They could have been kidnapped or killed. They could have committed suicide. The person could have also voluntarily made themselves "disappear" and assumed a new life in another location without notifying anyone.

In the cases I have worked, there have been many outcomes. Some missing persons have been found in the water, drowned, possibly indicating that they may have harmed themselves by committing suicide. Yet others have never been located.

I have a case study of one of these cases to share. I would like to take you through a journey where the perfect pre-meditated murder was disguised as a missing person case. The names and locations have been changed. As you will see, however, cold cases can be solved no matter when the incident occurred.

Before I begin, it is important to know the following facts about police procedure. To make an arrest there must be probable cause; reasonable belief that a person has committed a crime, based upon known facts. A "person of interest" to the police, is someone that is involved in a criminal investigation but was not formally charged with a crime. This person must be allowed to retain an attorney. The police cannot question that person if he/she has not been arrested; however, the individual may agree to be questioned by the police without a lawyer.

It all started one unseasonably warm Saturday, about 1:30 pm, at the end of October in the late 1990s. Robert Jones picked up Karen Mason[3] (both in their mid to late 20s) at her Bronx, NY, apartment. Robert had called Karen earlier that day. He said he was planning to leave home, and he wanted her to help him clean out his apartment. She would never return.

Karen was originally from the Midwest, and lived in New York City in an apartment with several roommates. Robert was a native New Yorker who lived in Brooklyn. Karen was five months pregnant at the time she disappeared. Karen was an honors student at a local college. Karen was seeing Robert, who was one of her professors. Robert had learned Karen was pregnant just days before he was scheduled to marry someone else. Karen was unaware of his other life with his fiancé. Robert had pleaded with Karen to get an abortion throughout her pregnancy, but she steadfastly refused.

When Karen didn't come home that night, her friends and family suspected the worst. Karen's sister, Kimberly, and Karen's roommate immediately thought Robert murdered Karen. Their suspicions were valid. Homicide is the leading cause of death among pregnant women.[4] Also, it was clear from the facts of the case that Robert was unhappy about Karen's pregnancy.

Kimberly and her family went to the police to report possible murder and file a missing person's report. The police didn't take the report until ten days later, when Kimberly had gone to the media and the event was covered extensively on television and in the newspapers.

Although the family identified the alleged killer to the police and had what they believed was circumstantial evidence of foul play, Robert retained an attorney and, from the outset, refused to cooperate. Kimberly believed that a perfect premeditated murder occurred—a murder in which no weapon, no physical evidence, no witnesses, no body and no smoking gun (something that would serve as conclusive evidence or proof of a crime) would ever be discovered.

Although the facts of the case were troubling, police were unable to investigate Robert's property for evidence. There was no probable cause—reasonable belief that a person has committed a crime, based upon known facts—under the Fourth Amendment to the U.S. Constitution. As a result, warrants could not be issued for search and seizure of his premises.

The case of Karen's disappearance was thus extremely difficult to pursue and solve. Robert didn't have to say anything to law enforcement due to his Miranda Warnings Rights. Under these rights, Robert could remain silent. Because of that, and the absence of probable cause, the investigation stymied law enforcement investigators for years, consequently giving the impression to the family that Robert had committed the perfect murder.

Overall, missing persons cases of this nature are extremely difficult to prosecute due to the lack of evidence and lack of a body. Although there have been cases that have been successfully prosecuted without a body, such cases are rare.

The family became frustrated with the criminal justice system and hired a private investigator. A private investigator can add value to these cases. What is the role of the private investigator? It's different from that of the police. The private investigator works with the family, understanding their feelings, emotions and expectations, and helps them best cope with the traumatic situation. This process can bring new facts and evidence to light. Kimberly later stated that the private investigation process "was the first time anyone gave Karen's closest friends and family a chance to share their views and opinions." The investigator intervenes and utilizes skilled techniques to help solve the crime and attempt to bring closure to the family. Ultimately, the family expects the private investigator to help find their missing person, dead or alive.

In this case, Kimberly hired a private investigator because she wanted to do everything possible to find her sister Karen. She said in an interview, "I would not abandon Karen," when announcing her decision to hire me. True to her word, she was very proactive when working with me. She was aggressive in following up on every lead regarding Robert, the Person of Interest in this case.

These cases take a lot of self-control on the part of the investigator. The investigator must take charge of the investigation and maintain a vision of the entire case, keeping an open mind to all possibilities. Upon initial involvement in a missing person case, the PI may listen or be guided by the family to immediately pursue their intentions. Families may want you to do things you are not comfortable with because of their primary focus, which may be on one person. It is essential that the private investigator be informed by, yet not guided by, the family. The PI must remain in charge of the investigation. That said, it is important for the investigator not to focus on any one suspect.

The PI must also perform a delicate balance, working as a private investigator alongside law enforcement. The PI must exercise a great amount of self-control in these situations. The PI is heavily involved in the case, yet fully understands his or her specific role. The private investigator does not parallel the actions of the police. Private Investigators are working with the family and have all the legal rights to conduct an investigation, unrelated to the work of the police. Ultimately, the police are the ones that analyze the evidence and make the arrest. The police and the private investigator cooperate with one another to arrive at the best investigative conclusion.

The family also plays a critical role in these cases. While the police will do their job and the private investigator does their job, ultimately, it is up to the family to keep the investigation active—especially when the case is assigned to the cold case squad.

In these cases, private investigators offer much-needed support, which can improve investigative outcomes. As discussed, these cases are emotionally draining. It can be difficult for families to navigate the criminal justice system. Many times, they are great investigative resources, yet they are unable to get the time with law enforcement they desire due to time constraints and competing priorities.

Thus, in this case, it was very important to interview the friends and family members extensively. I interviewed numerous people; way more than the police. When conducting interviews, investigators should utilize a proper listening technique. In this context, the ability to listen means not only listening to what a person has to say, but also paying attention to the person's body language, the tone of words spoken, being attentive, showing empathy, being aware of surroundings, and being sincere. These are some of the attributes that an effective and skilled investigator can use to elicit information.

The investigative process in this case was extensive. For example, I studied the customs of Robert and his family, I researched the possibility he hired a hitman (a hired killer), I visited several members of Robert's family, searched for Karen's body in waterways, dug in locations indicated by psychics, used extensive volunteers, among other techniques. I also made sure that Karen's case remained in the public view. Karen's case was featured on *48 Hours*, an hour-long cable TV documentary, and was featured in other news media.

In working almost from the inception of Karen's case, I was able to bring to light some very important information. I will share the investigative techniques I employed, as they may help other investigators better understand this type of investigative process. In all of these processes, teamwork and confidentiality are essential. You will also see the value of self-control on the part of the investigator when conducting these tasks. The investigative tasks I conducted were as follows:

■ Appeared on Major News Channels.
■ Communicated with law enforcement—a sensitive issue—yet avoided interfering with the police investigation.
■ Conducted approximately 150 interviews, both informational and as interrogations. Those interviews included inmates in prison and persons in homeless shelters. (It is important to note here that some of the subject's family were quite disrespectful, thus requiring a great deal of self-control in order to maintain proper composure.)
■ Conducted cell phone inspection.
■ Conducted ground searches, which included mapping out coordinates and creating specialized digging and search teams.
■ Conducted interviews of inmates in prisons and homeless shelters.
■ Conducted searches of countless areas of terrain, including waterways where divers were required.
■ Conducted surveillance.
■ Contacted local Senators, Assembly persons, politicians.
■ Created professional reports in a timely manner, used in court proceedings.
■ Distributed Flyers.
■ Documented pertinent information.
■ Employed new technology—cameras and cell phones.
■ Employed psychological techniques, such as understanding the psychological effects on the family of the victim.
■ Gathered evidence from the victim, including letters, journals, hair samples, dental X-rays, telephone numbers, appointments, meetings.
■ Organized a group of 200 search volunteers that included a diverse group of community members, from off-duty police officers to corporate CEOs.
■ Organized rescue searchers using specially trained search dogs.
■ Organized searches with the use of dogs.
■ Performed background checks and research on all individuals.
■ Prepared the case for eventual trial.
■ Searched for data in the victim's computer.
■ Understood the psychological effects on the "Person of Interest," and his/her family and friends.
■ Understood the psychological effects on the family of the victim.
■ Used psychological warfare (this concept involves actions intended to reduce an opponent's morale or mental well-being).

- ▪ Utilized innovative forensic technology.
- ▪ Utilized social media.
- ▪ Wrote press releases to major news channels.

Ultimately, we got a break in the case. Information was received by anonymous letters and phone calls to me and Kimberly, stating that two of Robert's family members may have been involved in helping Robert dispose of Karen's body. The family members were named. A background check revealed that one of Robert's relatives owned an auto body garage in Brooklyn. I checked and reviewed all of the businesses surrounding the garage and discovered that next to the garage was a large cement company. They informed me that they poured four inches of cement on the floor of the garage soon after Karen disappeared. I approached the owner and he would not let me search the garage, nor would he allow the police to search the garage for Karen's body or any DNA evidence. For the police, a subpoena is required, but because there was no probable cause, no subpoena was issued.

Later, additional information from anonymous sources stated that Karen was killed in the same Brooklyn auto body shop by Robert's named family members. However, this was not sufficient evidence for the police to obtain a search warrant and conduct a search. Again, I attempted to talk to the owner of the garage and asked him if I could conduct a search, but he refused. I also spoke to both of Robert's family members that were listed on the anonymous letters. They would not provide any information.

Finally, there was another development. The garage was sold. The new owners gave the police permission to dig to see if Karen's body may have been buried underneath the 4″ slab of cement. The police convened a contingent of professional experts. Bones were discovered, but they were not human bones. The publicity from the search reached Texas where Robert had established himself in a business with his family. Robert was exposed on the news, but there was still no probable cause to make an arrest.

One of the main ingredients for any investigator upon being involved in a missing person case with unusual circumstances is self-control. Years have passed, but Kimberly and I have never given up and have continued to pursue this case. Kimberly, although at times bewildered and exhausted by the constant march to find justice, will never give up until she finds her sister. When there is a missing person of this nature, where no body was recovered or found, the family has no closure. There is no place to pray or gravesite to visit. There is still uncertainty.

Despite our efforts, the case discovered no DNA, no weapon and no body. There was no probable cause. This case is now considered "cold," by definition, because it remains unsolved pending new evidence, and was assigned to the Cold Case Squad. It has been two decades, yet it is still an active case. Because this case involves a murder, and there is no statute of limitations limiting the prosecution for murder, the perpetrator can always be brought to justice. To this date, no arrest has been made due to the lack of probable cause. The body has never been recovered.

Due to the case still being active in the media by the family and the private investigator, tips still come in and are appreciated. These tips are acted upon by the police detective and the private investigator. Other anonymous tips have arrived and more searches have been conducted. The anonymous tips appear to be from family members describing detailed events that occurred in Karen's disappearance. Each tip has been followed up to this point. The police detective of the Cold Case Squad is still on the case and is very proactive. I, as the private investigator, have been sharing information with the detective.

Although there appears to be no end in sight, I believe that Karen's case can be solved. Anything can happen. There may be a confession by Robert's family members that they helped get rid of Karen's body; there may be a location where there is DNA. With the evolving state of technological advances, there is continued confidence that the case will one day be solved.

There have been a lot of recent advances that have assisted cold case investigations. Forensic technology and social media have revived many cases that were once considered cold. DNA technology has resulted in many of these cases being solved. We are now seeing cold cases being solved that occurred as long ago as 40 years.

For all types of casework, I have some advice for investigators when it comes to exercising self-control. First, some general advice. I suggest that you be very proactive. Do not sit back and wait for the evidence, data or information to come to you. It won't. Go out and seek information, pursue leads and be aggressive. Next, be sure to absorb all information gleaned, whether it appears important or not, at the time. It may have value as the investigation proceeds.

Finally, I have some advice pertaining to your subjects. I suggest that you refrain from focusing on one suspect, one scenario, one direction; instead, look at all peripheral information. In time, when you start to assemble the puzzle, all of the information gathered will start to make sense. Focusing on one subject limits your investigative focus and it also can hurt your case. There have been court cases where the investigators focused only on one person and, even if that was the person of interest, the courts have dismissed the case.

When conducting interviews of your subjects, be sure to organize your thoughts and prepare your questions beforehand. When asking questions, seek answers that will lead to other meaningful intelligence.

There might be times in your investigation when you lose self-control, especially when conducting complicated investigations, such as cold cases. There will come a time when things simply seem to fall apart. You may overreact, become overwhelmed, overcome, and anxiety will set in and control your thinking and behavior. For inexperienced investigators, there might appear to be no hope, because all leads have been exhausted; there seems to be nothing else to do, and you wish to quit—all self-control is lost.

In my cases, I am also challenged by victims' families' negative feelings towards law enforcement. It will take a lot of self-control to handle these situations. The families I work with are often frustrated by a perceived lack of communication from the police. Out of frustration, they might say that "cops don't know what they are doing" and the focus of their emotions generally turns to the direction of law enforcement. They will make strong statements, such as saying they hate all cops. Meanwhile they are expressing their negative feelings to me, a former police officer.

In these situations, I often feel compelled to defend the police. Consequently, I will become irritated and want to express my concerns. However, I always exercise self-control. I refrain from responding in an aggressive, agitated or angry way. During these times, I try to remember the following quote from Napoleon Hill: "No one can make you jealous, angry, vengeful, or greedy—unless you let him." Taking a deep breath and contemplating the circumstances, I realize that, without self-control, quitting can seem easy.

Over time, I realize victims' families' negative sentiments toward police are a part of their healing cycle. Over the years that I have been investigating missing person cases, I determined many families of missing persons will react to their situation by disliking the police. Families go through various emotions with the sudden loss of a loved one; they never said goodbye, they never said I love you, one last time. They also carry tremendous guilt that they could not prevent the incident. Often this cycle of emotions will result in anger and hate towards other parties, such as the police, then the anger will turn inwards, resulting in depression, and the cycle starts all over again.

In some missing persons cases I have investigated, it appears earlier police involvement would have been beneficial. There are instances where the police did not immediately take the case, even when the family was suspicious and believed that foul play was involved. The first few days someone is missing are critical to the investigation. I do not believe it is always prudent to wait 48 hours, as is sometimes recommended by law enforcement. Instead, this is the time when you need to push the investigation that much harder. Suddenly, new information will appear, not by luck, but by continuous hard work and diligence. In cases of persons who mysteriously disappear, or the perfect premeditated murder, there is most likely an attachment to the victim. Often the spouse or romantic partner is involved. A random killing is much more difficult to solve, because it is not as likely to be premeditated, nor is there an attachment to the victim.

There are a number of very important details to consider when accepting a missing person case. Self-control is critical in each of these points. First, treat the family with great respect, sensitivity, kindness, optimism, and professionalism. One should recognize the pain, emotional stress, and anguish with which they are living.

Next, remember you will not be able to take every case. As much as you want to help everyone, working with every family is not possible. Take only those cases where you feel as an investigator that you can add value. I assure each family that I work with, that I would not have taken the case if I were not confident that there would be some type of resolution. However, this belief does not come without hard work from the family and a real commitment from all parties. Keeping an optimistic attitude and imparting that attitude to the family is imperative.

The outcome of the case is also contingent upon the family's level of involvement. In my experience from working with families in crisis, I have found that family involvement is crucial to effective investigation and to bringing a resolution to these emotionally sensitive cases. Families must be involved in the actual investigation. This not only benefits the investigation, but also the family, as they feel involved and productive. By keeping them apprised of all developments, you enable them to feel somewhat in control in an otherwise uncontrollable situation. This allows families the freedom to be responsible for some aspects of the case.

The police are simply unable to maintain a certain level of family involvement. They have a strong need to maintain the integrity of their investigation and keep their information private. In conducting such cases, you must be cautious not to interfere with the investigation of the police department.

As evidenced in my case study, a great many interviews are conducted in missing persons investigations. There is certainly a strategy to how this process is conducted. My personal preference is to break the interviews into three parts. The first part is a "feeling out" period. The more homework the investigator does, and information he/she gathers prior to the interview, the more likely the questions are to be framed so that the final objective can be achieved. It is critical for the investigator to establish a bond of trust (not to be confused with friendship) with family members/friends of the missing person and/or the suspect.

No matter how much work you do to prepare, something can always go wrong. Here, self-control is necessary for success. The interviewee may refuse to talk, or never show up for the interview. You might get frustrated and angry when this happens. However, when that happens, relax and think of other options instead acting out or giving up. You will be more likely to think of a better technique if you remain calm.

Self-control can also help you succeed when questioning a subject. You want to remember to always learn more than you share in any exchange you have. If your subject is the perpetrator, or is involved with, or related in some capacity to the alleged suspect, they are just as curious as to what facts they are able to learn from you. Always keep this in mind so as not to divulge too much information. My approach is to have the person I am interviewing talk about themselves or something in common to both of us to build a rapport. Exercising patience, being calm and acting professionally relaxes the interviewee, thereby diffusing what might otherwise be a hostile environment.

Remember that the better you are at interviewing, the easier it will be. Over time, you will develop great confidence when conducting an interview. Once you have experience, knowledge and have acquired interviewing techniques, you will have total confidence you will be able to have a conversation with even the most unapproachable and hostile person.

A great interview is a process. It is important to use self-control and refrain from trying to achieve all of the objectives in one meeting. It can help to think from the perspective of the subject. Would you give all of your information to someone the first time you met them? It is significant for the investigator to realize that it is human nature not to tell a stranger (interviewer) everything at the first encounter, but obtaining trust is critical. At this stage, people are not candid; however, that has to be accepted in order to get on to the second phase.

It is easy to get angry during an interview. Some subjects can be frustrating to speak with, and when their statements contradict the truth it can be downright anger-inducing. The ability to control ones' emotions in this state is necessary. Verbally attacking the person being interviewed because he is lying leads to dead ends. Self-control is necessary for success.

The second phase of an interview begins when the interviewee responds to the questions asked. Typically, the subject will not tell the total truth. Subjects will often mix denials, half-truths or lies, along with the truth. This is the time when an investigator has to work really hard and be very cunning in their line of questioning in order to sift fact from fiction and truth from lies.

One way to foster a more truthful conversation is to employ active listening techniques. Investigators should research active listening techniques and use them during their interviews. Active listening involves showing interest in everything that the person expresses. The use of active listening techniques will help establish a bond between interviewer and interviewee. With effort, a working bond of trust should come out of this part of the interview process.

As an investigator, it is just as important to listen as it is to talk. The ability to listen while letting the person speak often leads to other important details. This is the one skill that separates an ordinary investigator from a great investigator: the ability to listen.

Finally, the objective of the third part of the interview is to eliminate the subject's fabricated responses, and concentrate on the truth. In this phase, you will decide exactly what you want to get out of the interview. This stage is where any critical information is shared. In terms of information sharing, investigators should share just enough that the subject realizes that you have done your homework. Be sure that their perception is that you have attained a great deal of knowledge about the case. Keep in mind that you may only have one chance for an interview, and if you alienate that one piece of indispensable communication, there may be no second opportunity. Finally, leave the person with a sense that you are able to return and re-interview them. Do not terminate the interview without coming away with other leads.

In these cases, there is a very high threshold for achievement. The families of missing persons are understandably desperate and could have unrealistic expectations. No matter how great your investigation might be, you may never fully satisfy your client. Bear in mind that with, or without self-control, no one, including the police, private investigators and court officials, may accomplish what the family of the missing demand. In this instance, it is important to keep the family focused on reality and keenly aware of your course of action. To maintain a healthy and productive working relationship, the PI needs to show empathy and learn and understand the personalities and the behaviors of the members of the family.

In this case, the family was happy with the final outcome. Although their loved one was not found, they know everything possible is being done to find her.

Investigators: Believe in Yourselves

There are many types of investigations. Once you determine your niche, you can capitalize on that talent. Some investigators may be adept at interacting with people, others may be better at confrontational interviews and obtaining confessions, others may be best at conducting background searches, writing reports, interacting with the media or surveillance. Your talent might be best served in the field of missing persons investigations, or in another investigative specialty area. There are also many investigative-related careers, such as investigative analysts and forensic accountants, crime scene evaluators, behavioral crime analysts and criminal profilers, just to name a few. Developing an awareness of your intrinsic motivation (your inner voice) will make you one of the best investigators in your specialty.

Notes

1. Merriam-Webster Dictionary.
2. Sanders, B. (2011) *Warrior Wisdom: Ageless Wisdom for the Modern Warrior*. Colorado: Kaizen Quest.
3. The names have been changed.
4. Cheng, D. and Horon I.L. (2010) *Obstetric Gynecology* 115(6): 1181–1186.

Chapter 3

Curiosity

Emmanuelle Welch

I am a naturally curious person. Tell me "I don't give a fig," or any of its more florid variations, and you'll inevitably leave me reaching for more. "What makes you say that?" I'd reply, hoping to jolt the conversation back to more fertile territory. I simply cannot understand what it's like to not be interested. I wonder about all the things that life serves us hot and crazy from the grill. And with the right disposition and/or social lubricant, I can drum up enthusiasm even for the most harrowing of topics—American football comes to mind.

My curiosity was likely piqued by my upbringing. I was raised in France, a nation that intrigued early twentieth century American novelist Edith Wharton for its "dauntless curiosity" and "perpetual desire for the new thing."[1] French public schools aim at widening children's curiosity, for the sake of enriching their background knowledge. Thus, I was exposed to a variety of disciplines, including Latin, philosophy and even the theory of knowledge, known as epistemology.

Copious material to feed my curiosity was also provided at home. Dinners with my educator parents and inquisitive brothers were confabs on any topic, from the Pompeii ruins to the star power of Freddie Mercury in the Communist Eastern bloc. Visitors drawn by my mother's cooking would tell stories of being caught in the middle of the Iranian Revolution or working archaeological sites in Ethiopia. A bespectacled, introverted kid, I would soak up the atmosphere until I could muster the courage to ask questions. At 22, I took off to become a foreign correspondent in various countries, then, in my 30s, I became a private investigator.

Luckily, a boundless sense of curiosity about the world is the bedrock personality trait for my chosen professions. Perhaps this is why I was drawn to these fields. Both journalists and investigators are driven by an instinctive need to know the story behind the story. Both are propelled by the higher calling of finding the truth. I have found in the 15 years I have owned my investigative business that the best investigators are skilled at asking questions, they listen well, and, when they run into a brick wall, take delight in figuring out how to get around it.

Learning how to harness, develop, and extend natural curiosity is critical to becoming a great investigator. Luckily, a sense of curiosity can be honed in anyone. Curiosity guru Brian Grazer, the spiky-haired and wildly successful Hollywood producer, says that each of us is born hardwired to seek out stimulation and knowledge. Grazer's own curiosity culminated in a lifelong habit of conducting "curiosity interviews" with select celebrities. He writes about this experience in his best-selling book *A Curious Mind*. Overall, he equates curiosity with power, and finds it never truly goes away, just lies dormant sometimes, always standing at the ready to be re-awakened and unleashed.

Curiosity is an important skill for investigators, who need to elicit information from people in order to succeed. The key question is: are you curious? Behavioral scientist Dr. Robert Maurer finds that most people think they are curious, when in reality, they are just asking questions. In fact, when Maurer asks people if they are curious, they invariably say "yes," yet as a practical matter he finds true curiosity to be rare. He theorizes that people whose job involves asking customers or clients questions confuse their interactions with a genuine sense of discovery: "Whether you are a physician, a mechanic, a salesperson, or wait staff, asking questions is a necessary problem-solving skill," Mauer wrote in his blog, *The Traits of Excellence*,[2] "however, problem-solving should not be confused with true curiosity." The same applies to professional investigators.

However, the challenge for investigators is that people do not always want to talk to them, and the investigator may not always be naturally interested in the subject matter at hand. Yet Maurer finds that people can hone their natural sense of curiosity by asking questions in such a way to elicit emotion and get people to speak enthusiastically. For example, he says to ask questions such as "Could you help me to understand, what are your thoughts about …", "How do you feel about …" or "How do you respond to people who say …" or "Please tell me more about…." This way, everyone remains interested and engaged and a true information exchange takes place.

Although there are many tools to assist the investigator in developing a sense of curiosity, many believe true curiosity isn't self-conscious. Philosopher H.S. Broudy discussed this position in his work "Disinterested curiosity and social concern"[3] where he said curiosity isn't selective. It is not a tool for endearing yourself to people. Instead, it's disinterested, it's free. As the British science writer Philip Ball elegantly said, "True curiosity grinds to a halt when deprived of wonder's fuel."

Curiosity Knocking

Sincere curiosity is a tangible advantage in "old gumshoe" types of investigations requiring legwork, door-knocks and human connection. As Grazer notes, "Authentic human connection requires curiosity." These cases tend to be less frequent in my business in New York City, where a lot of the work is white collar, often involving stealth intelligence gathering. I encounter more and more attorneys or clients asking the investigator not to contact anyone during their research; not even a city clerk to help locate a public record! But there is one primary type of investigation that can be dubbed the "bagel and cream cheese" of many New York City private Investigators (PIs), often calling for in-depth human interaction: The Landlord Tenant investigation, or L&T.

L&T investigations are very popular in New York City. Here, with a skyrocketing rental market, skewed by a large proportion of rent-controlled or rent-regulated apartments, some tenants turn their digs into cash cows. This behavior is illegal in New York City. Thus, landlords hire PIs to document clandestine apartment-based businesses, such as massage parlors, and illegal sublets. Sleuths also perform "intelligence mining" for landlords who want to buy reluctant tenants out of their leases on the most favorable possible terms.

During undercover AirBnB stays or pretext encounters, where investigators gather initial information, curiosity goes a long way. A curious investigator can turn small talk with a targeted tenant into a meaningful conversation. Contrary to popular belief, investigating tenants suspected of illegal activities doesn't always work to their disadvantage.

In one such case, I was serving as the undercover investigator in an L&T matter. In this capacity, I rented a room in Manhattan for less than $80 a night. The tenant of this rent-stabilized apartment, a bartender, was no longer on speaking terms with his landlord, and was late on his rent. He had a European wife and a beautiful new baby. The wife looked miserable, and I could see that she loathed having strangers stay over, while she tiptoed around trying to rock her newborn to sleep. As a mother and an immigrant myself, I was curious to know what was going through her mind.

I decided to use that curiosity to further my investigation. I initiated a conversation with her husband over a morning coffee. He revealed she was very homesick. Her American dream? A house in New Jersey. She wanted to move, and he was resisting. Like so many New Yorkers before him, this bartender was holding on to his rent-stabilized apartment because he felt he could never leave such a great deal behind. But deep inside, he had grown to hate the daily hustle of living in Manhattan. Our conversation gave me fascinating insight into the mind of a native New Yorker who desperately wanted to move, but felt pressured to stay, because quitting "the greatest city on Earth" felt like a failure.

In this case, my curiosity actually led to a great outcome for this subject. At the end of breakfast, he thanked me for my interest and I told him the truth—that I found the psychological ramifications of New York real estate fascinating and that I truly enjoyed chatting with him. My investigative report tried to flesh out the tenant as a human being facing all these paradoxes, and the last I heard, the landlord was no longer pursuing an eviction, but instead was trying to negotiate a buyout.

Are there ways to become more curious? In my case, my profession increased my natural sense of curiosity. I was lucky to work for many years as a journalist, which allows you to learn things in brand new fields every day. "Curiosity coaches" similarly recommend you amass all sorts of knowledge from which you can draw unthinkingly and spur still more curiosity. To this end, I read diverse kinds of newspapers and magazines. Reading books stimulates your mind through the minds of others. I also live my life with great enthusiasm. I don't take anything for granted, and truly enjoy learning about even the smallest facts in life. And I am careful to not let myself fall into the rut of routine, the number one enemy of curiosity.

Experts have suggested various methods to increase one's sense of curiosity. Gregory F. Treverton recommends looking at investigations as mysteries, rather than puzzles. As such, he recommends not trying to solve everything and instead to define the ambiguities.[4] Similarly, public records research master Don Ray (who is, incidentally one of the most inquiring investigators I've ever had the pleasure to train with), approached public-records hunting and gathering as an analytical process, as opposed to a simple fact-gathering mission. A people person, Ray would "interview" government-issued documents as if they were individuals in front of him. Some questions in his document interview framework are cheeky and thus memorable: "Who's your daddy?" (Find out who created the document and why.) "Are you really a blonde?" (Make sure someone hasn't altered the document.) "What other secrets are you keeping?" (Look for codes and fine prints.)

Curiosity Crowd-sourcing

Facebook's reputational issues in 2018 offered an interesting opportunity for investigators to test their sense of curiosity, especially those of us who specialize in Open Source Intelligence (OSINT). What is OSINT, exactly? There are as many definitions as there are investigators, but security consultant Justin Seitz came up with a perfectly simple one, calling it

> a process that involves utilizing open sources of information on the Internet, not just Twitter or Facebook, but also all sorts of things: Photographs of a location, an online article.... Pretty much anything that you can access online that doesn't involve clandestine sources and secrecy.[5]

Since the early aughts, OSINT and social media in particular have revolutionized the way investigations are conducted. Cases that don't involve at least one element of social media are rare. I often use social media to gather evidence in my cases. More recently, I had a workers' compensation scam artist who was posting on his main Facebook page sad selfies of himself wearing a neck brace, while simultaneously publishing videos on a "secret" Facebook account of him dancing and bopping his head in rhythm. I also investigated a New York City tenant who had turned his loft into a clandestine rehab facility for sex addicts, while unaware that his guests celebrated their "serenity journey to recovery" on social posts discoverable by geolocation.

One of my favorite social media cases was that of a French embezzler. He essentially assisted me with his own investigation. He was hiding in plain sight in Florida. There, he was posting pictures on Instagram from his waterfront condo, displaying his numerous hot rods, purchased with his ill-gotten gains. The pictures displayed the license plates, which I was able to match up to his DMV (Department of Motor Vehicles) records, pulled by my court runner, making for easy tracking. What's not to love!

OSINT investigators are especially interested in this type of evidence. They keep abreast of the latest investigative techniques to capture it. Many participate in forums, listen to specialty podcasts,[6] keep up with blogs,[7] follow Twitter feeds, join chat platforms, register for webinars and attend conferences such as OsmosisCon. This is vital to stay in the loop, as Murphy's Law very much applies to OSINT: you can be sure that any investigative procedure or tool created to facilitate online investigations (often programs written in Python) do wonders one day but will stop working or get pulled when you least expect it.

Recently, it has become harder to do these types of investigations. Revelations about "fake news" emanating from Russian troll farms, plus online privacy concerns fueled in part by the Cambridge Analytica scandal, led to Facebook taking measures against many search functions enjoyed by OSINT analysts. In June 2019, Facebook quietly disabled a set of advanced features that were allowing investigators to deep-dive into the social network in powerful ways.[8] Facebook's changes rendered numerous methods and tools obsolete overnight. Professional investigators, law enforcement, journalists and non-government organizations (NGOs) reacted with shock, if not outrage: "Facebook just blindfolded war crimes investigators" lamented Amnesty International's Sam Dubberley. Amid various scandals and breaches, other social media sites such as Instagram and LinkedIn have also erected obstacles to their search functions. Governments enact legislation that has a domino-effect on OSINT investigations, such as the General Data Protection Regulation (GDPR) in the European Union. Aimed at restricting the processing of personal data, this regulation has scared internet registrars around the world. Many have decided to hide information on domain name owners from the public database known as WHOIS, thus making it more difficult to identify the people behind a website. As Germany-based intelligence analyst Matthias Wilson put it: "The Golden Age of OSINT is over."[9]

As frustrating as these disruptions are, they remind researchers to never assume everything they can do today will work tomorrow. Investigators are wise to continue to seek alternate research methods. This is where curiosity comes in. "If you're a good investigator, you're gonna be curious by nature," Justin Seitz told listeners on the Privacy, Security, & OSINT Show. He continued,

> Take that curiosity, take a little bit of tenacity, look exactly at what you're trying to do, and hit your head against the wall for many hours until something works. You spend hours on top of years of experience in order to figure that technique out.

While Seitz was speaking in jest, the message is clear—the curious investigator will utilize multiple avenues of research and will eventually get the job done.

OSINT investigators heed the calling. Whenever an online search trick gets removed from their toolkits, members of the OSINT community start poking around with palpable thrill. They swap suggestions on forums or on Twitter on how to circumvent the new obstacle and "look under the hood" of web pages and social media networks. They exchange feedback on methods tested on burner phones or virtual machines, which are an emulation of a computer system or mobile operating system within your computer. London terrorism OSINT analyst Loránd Bodó wrote a short guide on how to remain "OSINT curious" by educating oneself on the work fellow OSINT investigators are doing. Per Bodo, there is no shortage of materials, because "There are many brilliant OSINTers out there, sharing their insights and knowledge with the broader community."[10]

This exchange is welcomed, yet it is not the norm in the investigative community. To be clear, sharing information and knowledge isn't often the default position for investigators. This is a profession that likes to cultivate secrecy, certainly from the general public but also among colleagues, except in selected settings such as association dinners or conferences. One of my investigative mentors, a Los Angeles private eye who grew up as a performing child magician, would keep his cards close to the vest, literally, though that didn't prevent him from being a generous teacher behind closed doors. A Murphy door, in fact. When I attended his detective academy, the school was hidden in the back of a locksmith and hardware store, accessible by pushing a revolving wall panel!

Generally, there's somewhat of a culture gap between traditional investigators and the new crop of OSINT investigators. They tend to live by the Creative Commons motto: "When we share, everyone wins." The new generation doesn't think twice about crowd-sourcing their curiosity on repositories, inspired by the open-mindedness of experts such as Michael Bazzell, a former police detective and FBI analyst founder of the IntelTechniques[11] community. Army veteran and Open Source Intelligence consultant Kirby Plessas,[12] and software engineer Irina Shamaeva,[13] are also leading lights in this community. In the new game of cat and mouse, investigators and analysts are banding together to solve challenges thrown in by big data providers such as Google, Facebook, Amazon and LinkedIn.

Hacking the Dating Apps

Interest is often mistakenly interpreted as intelligence. Yet my own modest contribution to the OSINT community's toolbox is proof that any investigator can innovate, as long as they apply a little curiosity. In 2017, I noticed that more "Joe Suspects" and "Jane Subjects" were becoming less active on social media. They were either neglecting their social media accounts or locking them with the highest privacy settings, making them more difficult to investigate. If Facebook use is slowing down and if people are setting their Instagram accounts to "private." What is the next frontier? I could befriend a target on social media, but that is taboo for the type of cases that I work on, except in potentially life-threatening situations such as child abductions.

Naturally my curiosity was piqued. What is next? I was reading more and more about dating meet-up and hook-up apps, and the privacy concerns they were raising. I decided to try locating one of my "skips" (skip tracing investigation subjects, who cannot be contacted via telephone, mail or in person) on an app aimed at gay men. Sure enough, the same guy who was on the "downlow" on a restricted Facebook account was on Grindr soliciting new friends! I realized that dating apps were these people's weakest links. Even while keeping a low profile in real life, they were still trying hard to find a partner. They wanted to be found! Not by investigators, of course, but there they were in all their glory: bathroom selfies, "headless torsos," the "who is who?" group photo, and more.

I realized this was a great source of information for OSINT investigators. Wonder, curiosity's mercurial sibling, has never ceased to amaze me, when it comes to dating apps. Let's just say that they teleport me into exotic subcultures very remote from my daily reality. I started downloading and testing apps, and working out ways to game the scenes of Tinder, Grindr, OK Cupid, Plenty of Fish, Craigslist, and specialized sites (fetish and lifestyle forums) to locate and investigate people. Intrigued by the different "hacks" available on Github to search better within those apps, I hired a French-American science major who had explored the Tinder Application Programming Interface (API) as a hobby and knew how to code in Python. He built a custom tool to refine searches within Tinder and increase the chances of getting results more likely to contain a target's profile. I also started building a public repository of dating and hook-up apps[14] and the research around them.

I became a go-to investigator in the OSINT community, based on these skills and data. As word spread that I was "into dating apps," I was invited to give a presentation at the Third Osmosis Conference, the annual online social media and open-source intelligence gathering created by the original "cyber librarian" turned private investigator and OSINT trainer, Cynthia Hetherington. "Let's enjoy it while it lasts," I told attendees, warning them that, just as social media had erected barriers against abuse, dating sites were implementing anti-catfishing measures and other hurdles to investigators.

My ideas proved to be novel. Many told me afterwards that, because they never worked on infidelity cases, they hadn't thought of utilizing these sites and apps to locate people, learn about their place of employment, investigate assets. While this was not rocket science, it was a unique research technique that has proven useful to many investigators.

Life is more interesting to the interested investigator, but unbridled curiosity also has its perils. Dig too deeply and you may end up doing regrettable things. The curious investigator needs to keep some discretion and hold things back; some things are really better left unexplored or unsaid!

In one case, my curiosity led me to more information than I had bargained for. I once worked on a genealogy case between France and the United States. Over the course of my research, I located a long-lost relative of the client! I was so thrilled to locate this person that I kept the initial conversation going perhaps a little longer than I should have. While it is said that curiosity comes from intentional pauses, the silence allowed this relative to spill family secrets involving the client that I wish I had never heard.

Another dark side of curiosity is perilous decision making. An April 2016 study on curiosity by Hsee and Ruan,[15] described the potential harmful outcomes of curiosity and the desire to resolve uncertainty, despite negative consequences. As any OSINT investigator who spends time in the depths of the dark web can tell you, it is unwise to wander from one ".onion" web site to another out of sheer curiosity, at the risk of getting your computer infected by malware or potentially seeing "things that you can't unsee" in the depths of the dark web.

Nevertheless, a truly curious person doesn't let past hurts affect their future. The curious investigator is wise to move forward and start over. However, this is not the easiest path to take, because people tend to dwell on the past. According to psychotherapist David Klow, "The problem for many adults is that we stop being curious about new experiences and are instead focused on understanding what we've already been through."[16] Indeed, curious investigators continually develop a strong base, investigate new options, forcing themselves beyond the comfort zone. They walk the fine line between learning from their mistakes and remaining eager to taking risks. One key, I found, is to share discoveries with fellow investigators who support our explorations and reciprocate. Their validation makes us more curious and their interest fuels our persistence. My investigative partner, Bill Golodner, a retired NYPD detective turned private investigator, always lends an ear and helps me almost relish the uncertainty: "You don't need all of the answers right now. Let fun last."

Notes

1. Edith Wharton (1919) *French Ways and Their Meaning* (New York: Countryman Press, 1977).
2. www.psychologytoday.com/us/blog/the-traits-excellence/201704/the-power-curiosity.
3. *The Journal of Higher Education*, 14(8) (1943), pp. 426–430.
4. "Risks and Riddles" *Smithsonian Magazine*, June 2007.
5. Podcast, Justin Seitz, The Privacy, Security & OSINT Show, October 2018.
6. The Privacy, Security, & OSINT Show: https://inteltechniques.com/podcast.html; https://osintcurio.us.
7. https://medium.com/week-in-osint.
8. www.vice.com/en_us/article/zmpgmx/facebook-stops-graph-search.
9. https://keyfindings.blog/2019/01/04/the-golden-age-of-osint-is-over/.
10. https://osintcurio.us/2019/01/22/five-things-you-can-do-to-stay-osint-curious/.

11. https://inteltechniques.com/menu.html.
12. https://plessas.mykajabi.com/.
13. https://booleanstrings.com/.
14. https://start.me/p/VRxaj5/dating-apps-and-hook-up-sites-for-investigators.
15. "The Pandora Effect: The Power and Peril of Curiosity," *Journal of Psychological Science*, March 21, 2016.
16. www.fastcompany.com/3045148/8-habits-of-curious-people.

Chapter 4

Patience

Tom Martin

By definition, patience is "the capacity to accept or tolerate delay, trouble, or suffering without getting angry or upset".[1] In this chapter, the breadth and value of patience in an investigator will be discussed from the perspective of this career investigator. For an investigator working major case investigations, the quality of patience takes many forms. Here are a few examples. There is the patience involved when taking your time and doing your job to the best of your ability. The patience involved when waiting for search warrants to be drafted and signed by a judge. Being patient when allowing a suspect the chance to speak. (That is, the person seated in the interview chair who is coming up with the most outrageous story you have ever heard, and he expects you to believe it. In this case, just listen, and be patient. Allowing him to speak may allow him one opportunity to slip and reveal something that he otherwise intended to keep inside.) There is patience required to continually reassess the job at hand as new information develops. The need to be patient with supervisors who want answers before the investigator is done evaluating and assessing. The need to be patient with opposing attorneys who will always manage to find fault with something in your case file, and will liberally sling derogatory comments at you and your work. The ability to be patient with family members and understand their frustrations with your long hours at work, when your cases aren't progressing quickly enough. Finally, there is patience required to explain investigative concepts to a layperson, such as the difference between a suggestion of involvement and admissible evidence. It takes evidence to bring a case to trial … not a feeling that "I just know he did it." The virtues of patience in an investigator will be illustrated in this work, which documents some of my most memorable investigative experiences.

Career Path

I never planned to work in forensic science and crime scene investigation, but I always wanted to be a New York State Trooper. I grew up about 100 yards from the local barracks. I was always around state troopers. They presented well. Intimidating at times, but always professional. They always seemed in control, able to handle anything. I always knew that's what I wanted to be when I grew up.

The first day I entered the New York State Police Academy I learned why they presented so well … the hard way. The academy was absolutely brutal. Six months of everything from classroom instruction to physical training to defensive tactics training, to a complete overall attitude adjustment. The days were long. They usually started about 5:00 am with physical training followed by a five-mile run around the college campus next door. After breakfast there was four hours of classroom instruction, lunch, four more hours of class instruction and then defensive tactics training before dinner. After dinner we were locked in our dorm rooms for two hours for what was called mandatory study. There was a test every week, if you failed more than one … you were out. Dismissed from the academy. The worst part of the day were the hours that followed mandatory study. This session began at 9:00 pm and ended whatever time they decided to let us go to bed; usually between 11:00 pm and midnight. This was the session or training that adjusted your attitude and made you more stress tolerant. It usually involved exhaustive physical training (after a day that was already 16 hours long, and counting) with a whole lot of screaming and yelling involved. In retrospect, it was tough, but I'm glad I went through it.

In basic training, I learned that patience in a patrol officer is an extremely valuable quality. A patient officer will demonstrate increased planning, wherever possible, when conducting activities. This gives the officer a better chance of doing things right, the first time. (There isn't always a second chance, in policework.) Patient officers will also be well-equipped to diffuse difficult situations that can arise without notice. As a patrol officer, I learned it is difficult to predict the behavior of the public. As a result, the street officer never knows if he might be dealing with an emotionally disturbed person (EDP), violent individual or a regular citizen having a bad day. The responding officer needs to have the patience to evaluate the situation and make the best choice. There is little room for error, and mistakes can be dangerous.

My forensic career began completely by happenstance. I was still a uniformed road trooper with about two years of service when I was asked if I would be interested in becoming a field crime scene technician or CST. Field CSTs were trained in basic crime scene investigation and handled less serious offenses such as burglaries, larcenies, and vehicle collisions. When positions opened up in the forensic crime scene unit, personnel were chosen from these field positions. I decided to pursue this career path.

I went into that forensic unit two years later, with about four years under my belt as a uniformed road trooper. I stayed in that unit for the remainder of my career; 18 years total, with 14 as the supervisor. In this unit, my responsibilities included forensic investigations of violent crimes.

Every day that I went to work in that unit, I got to witness first-hand the absolute worst that this world had to offer. Children murdered by their parents and care takers. Women murdered by their husbands or boyfriends after suffering years of chronic abuse. Gang members who tortured and mutilated each other to send a message as to how vicious they could be if you crossed them. I witnessed people being shot, stabbed, strangled, and suffocated. I've seen human beings who were decapitated, dismembered, and disemboweled. I also spent time during the recovery operations at ground zero following the attacks of 9/11 and the subsequent investigation into anthrax that was being sent through the mail shortly after those attacks. I've been asked many times what it's like to deal with such horrors on a regular basis. The answer is simple. It's a routine part of your job. You become desensitized to it when you see it constantly. Nothing shocks me anymore. As a professional task, investigations look to find truth through objectivity. Emotions interfere with objectivity, so you have to leave your emotions at home.

When I started out I was sent to training class after training class to learn forensic crime scene investigation. Everything from basic crime scene protocols and procedures and evidence collection, to specialized fields such as fingerprint identification, bloodstain pattern analysis, and shooting reconstruction. I was even trained as a forensic composite sketch artist. I couldn't draw a stick figure before my training in that field, but I eventually learned to draw faces of unknown persons as they were described to me by eye witnesses.

Composing composite sketches from a witness's memory was an exercise in patience. The process took hours and involved asking the victim or witness to re-live the event. Specific information was needed to compose a sketch, but often times the victim or witness would only catch a quick glimpse of the offender. It was a process to capture the witness's memory and translate that image to paper. It also involved constantly ensuring that we were on the same page, in terms of the description. Sketches often require copious editing before they were complete. Ultimately, the composite sketch had to reflect the witness's memory, not the artist's convenience. It's an exercise in patience to coordinate that effort. You could often measure the accuracy of the composite from the victim's reaction to the final sketch. The more accurate the sketch, the more emotional the victim would usually become.

One of the first things one learns in forensic investigation training is how slow-moving and methodically a case progresses. This teaches you the value of patience. When you watch an investigative show on television, they have to fit the entire storyline in the time slot allotted to that particular show, so things tend to move quickly. In the real world, cases progress a lot more slowly. You have to take your time. That goes with anything, from scene investigations, to interviewing victims, witnesses, and suspects, to pouring through thousands of phone records or financial receipts. You can't rush a good job.

Patience during the Investigation

Television programming gives the false perception that homicide and violent crime cases can be solved each and every time, in about 40 minutes or so (one-hour program minus commercials). During the 40 minutes that it takes to solve a case on TV, there is non-stop action, excitement, intrigue, and drama. That couldn't be further from the truth in the reality of crime scene investigation. Not only does it take great deal of time and resources to investigate violent crimes, it also takes great patience.

Once an investigation commences—after the initial call for help subsides, and the scene is secured—things tend to move quite slowly. Just the initial arrival on scene can take hours. Briefings take place, investigators wait for the arrival of additional or specialized personnel, medical examiners and their investigators, and further wait the eternity that it often takes to draft search warrants. In real crime scene investigation, there is rarely a rush.

In the many years I have been teaching crime scene investigation, I have had the opportunity to speak to undergrad students studying forensic science and crime scene investigation. New investigative students are often surprised to learn that crime scene investigations can be tedious, unglamorous and unexciting, unlike the way they are portrayed in the media. Indeed, from my experience, crime scene investigation is dirty, tiresome, monotonous, painstakingly slow, and often comes with a variety of offensive odors. The dividend comes eventually in the form of figuring out the mystery. When the pieces of the puzzle are properly assembled and the answer is revealed, the investigator is rewarded. The student or new investigator needs to be aware the effort involves patience rather than glamour. The absence of glamour tends to turn away many aspiring young investigators. (Ultimately, those who are turned away from the realities are probably best suited for other fields.)

At any given scene, there is a lot of work to be done on the part of the investigator. Photographs are taken, notes and visual observations are recorded, and the scene is diagramed in order to show the spatial relationships between items and areas. Numerous measurements are taken and recorded in order to produce scale diagrams. Some of these tasks have been made simpler with modern technology, but most of it is accomplished the old-fashioned way, with a pencil and a notepad.

Finally, physical evidence in different forms will be collected. Some of this evidence is deemed to be "scientific," it will be analyzed in a laboratory. Other evidence will be collected to help investigators reconstruct events and tell the story.

The process of evidence collection can take a lot of patience on the part of the investigator. The rule of thumb in evidence collection is that "It's better to have it and not need it, than to need it and not have it." In the early stages of an investigation, information is minimal, so when it's not clear what might be important, everything becomes important. The tendency is collect far more evidence than might be necessary, just in case. This comes with issues as well. First, the agency collecting the evidence will need sufficient space to store everything. Most evidence, once collected, will be maintained for many years. In a murder case, it may be retained for the life of the accused, if he or she is convicted.

Government crime laboratories are tremendously backlogged with analyses. Most crime labs will only allow a certain number of items to be submitted for testing. Therefore, if the police agency collects 100 items of evidence, the lab may only test ten of them. The fact is that most of those additional items of evidence are superfluous. They are collected just in case. Again, "It's better to have it and not need it, than to need it and not have it".

Evidence collection can certainly test the patience of any investigator. Take bloodstains for an example. Bloodstains at a given crime scene are often depicted as sensational pieces of evidence, and to an extent that may be true. However, it's not enough to understand the dynamics of blood in motion, and how bloodstains are created, it's equally important to identify the source of those bloodstains. This is accomplished by collecting bloodstains or bloodstained items from throughout the scene.

The more bloodstains that are found at the scene, the more involved the collection of bloodstains becomes. In a murder case involving multiple blunt force trauma there may be many thousands of individual blood spatters or blood stains present. Not all will be swabbed. Decisions will need to be made as which stains will be swabbed based upon information that includes, but is not necessarily limited to, the location, direction, type of stain, distribution pattern, etc. The source of the blood at the scene will need to be identified. This is accomplished through DNA testing of blood swabs or bloodstain evidence associated with the scene.

The process of entering a bloodstain into evidence will demonstrate the patience involved in evidence collection. Each bloodstain is first photographed with the entirety of the scene, then as a specific group, and finally close up so that the stains can be analyzed and described later. After being photographed, each stain to be collected must be marked, indicated and described on a corresponding diagram, measured from one or more points of reference, and finally swabbed onto an approved laboratory swab conducive to DNA analysis. After swabbing, each stain is allowed to air dry before being placed into a box, then into an envelope, and marked before being cataloged as evidence. This process can take hours or even days, depending on the complexity of the scene and the number of samples to be tested. It's anything but exciting. It requires patience.

One objective of collecting bloodstains is to determine which stains more likely came from the bleeding victim, and which more likely originated from an injured offender. Depending on the circumstances of the case, and the location in which the bloodstains were discovered, a single bloodstain from an offender or a victim may help in solving a case. Identifying particular types of bloodstains found on scene are part of the investigative process. This can sometimes be akin to finding a needle in a haystack if there is an extraordinary amount of bloodstains present. Patience is required in not only documenting and collecting bloodstain samples, but in triaging those bloodstains in order to determine which are likely to be the most probative.

The reality is that this task cannot be achieved in the time allotted to a television program, which is why the real job is very different from the one depicted in the media.

The time and patience investigators spend in conducting thorough evidence collection often yields fruitful results in the case. Perpetrators of violent crimes tend to watch television too. Many put the skills they have learned from their favorite investigative TV show to practice when altering or destroying scene evidence. But critical bloodstain evidence may still be left behind. Why? People who have it in their heart to violently kill another human being rarely burden themselves with being careful. When the blunt or sharp object is being swung into the victim with such force and ferocity, the offender often loses track of where the left hand is located while the right hand is swinging. At other times the victim may be able to deliver one solid strike to the nose of the offender causing a profuse nose bleed. Active bleeding from the offender at the crime scene is often very compelling evidence, but doesn't jump out in obvious fashion as is depicted on television. It takes perseverance and patience to identify and recover that evidence.

Patience after the Investigation

The patience involved in investigations isn't limited to documenting and collecting evidence. It extends to criticisms that most of the time are the result of insufficient information. It can take a patient investigator to both process a scene and also to hear criticism of their work. When cases go unsolved, the police investigators are often blamed. Phrases such as "The police screwed up the crime scene" or "The police really did a lousy job on this one" are phrases I have heard over and over again. The translation of these statements, and others like them, is: *there is something about the scene that I would like to see or know, and the information I require has not been documented by the scene investigators.*

It's true that not all crime scene investigations are perfect, but few investigations are the abominations that some might suggest. The fact is that investigators have limited and minimal information available to them while at the crime scene. The crime scene is usually released long before the investigation ends. As new information develops, the relevance of a particular piece of evidence or a photograph of a particular area may suddenly become important. If it's missing from the case file, it's not because the investigator ignored it, or missed it. Most of the time, the information that it might be important was not available.

It's frustrating to hear attorneys, both prosecutors and defense, as well as peers, supervisors, etc., criticize investigators for "leaving something out." These "omissions" are most often not intentional, it's simply a result of the CSI not having the luxury of having months-worth of information after the scene has been released. Investigators must patiently process this information, with the understanding that most people are unaware of the complexities they face in evidence collection.

Case Study

Police agencies nationwide constantly struggle with balancing limited personnel and minimal budgets to work extremely important cases. I suppose that I always knew of this situation but I experienced it first-hand during a serial killer investigation.

A serial killer I will call Ken, lived with his parents and a younger sibling in a home on a crowded city street, directly across the street from a busy medical park and only a few blocks away from an Ivy League college. Over a period of approximately 22 months, Ken murdered eight women. He manually strangled them. What's more, he stashed their bodies in his home, to decompose for as long as 22 months. The first five victims were kept in the attic, and the last three in the crawlspace under the house. That's right—in the home he shared with his parents and younger sibling. While it may seem unfathomable that anyone could secrete eight bodies in their residence without other family members being aware of those decomposing bodies, one must understand the everyday condition of the home.

One of the things that an investigator learns early in his career is that not all people live in clean sanitary homes; the state in which some people choose to live is disturbing. An investigator learns quite a bit about an individual when searching their home. Visual observations of what hangs on the walls in the home, or sits on the bookshelves, gives a quick understanding of that homeowner's personality, interests, hobbies, etc. Some homes are kept immaculate, and look freshly cleaned. Some are neat and tidy, but less clean. That is, everything is properly put away in its place, but the home has very apparently not been vacuumed, wiped, or dusted for some time. Other homes are quite unclean, with visible insects, rodents, rodent droppings, and worse. Some homes literally have no area on the floor upon which one could comfortably walk from one area to another—the floors are just cluttered with debris. Messy homes are not uncommon to a crime scene investigator. This serial killer's home however, was in a class all by itself.

When we first arrived at the home to execute the search warrant, it seemed as though all of the flies occupying that house were trying to get *out*. That's about how bad it was. To say that the home was in a state of disrepair would be the understatement of the century. There was garbage everywhere. Kitchen garbage piled up in covered porches. Grease and grime covered nearly everything. Boxes of clutter in nearly every room. And an odor that I couldn't describe. Essentially, the everyday condition in which the home was kept, seemed to mask the smell of eight decomposing corpses.

Every investigator who has ever worked a death scene knows the smell of human decomposition. It's a distinct odor all unto itself. If you've never come in contact with it, I wouldn't be able to describe it to you. But once you've experienced the odor of decomposing human remains, you never forget it. It is unmistakable. And the second you set foot into Ken's home, it punched you right in the nose. There are decomposing bodies in this house.

Ken's eight victims were all reported to be missing. The list grew over that 22-month period. A missing person task force had been assembled at the request of the district attorney. Detectives from several police agencies and the DA's office were dedicated to do nothing else but find the cause of the women going missing. FBI behavioral analysts or "profilers" were brought in to assist.

The case broke when Ken assaulted one woman whom he eventually let go. She immediately sought help and implicated Ken as her attacker. Information from this victim led to the information and evidence that produced the search warrant on his home. Ken confessed to the murders prior to the execution of the warrant. He identified the women he murdered and told us that we would find five bodies in his attic and three in the crawlspace under the house. He swore up and down that his parents and sibling knew nothing of the bodies decomposing in the home. No charges were ever brought against any of his family members.

While Ken's confession was a good start, he threw us a bit of a surprise. One of the women that Ken confessed to killing, was *not* on our missing persons list. She had been reported missing two counties away, and the connection was never made. Therefore, Ken effectively, in his confession, gave us a ninth missing person and only indicated that there were eight bodies in his home. The victim who was on our missing persons list who Ken denied killing has not been found to this date. She was not located on the property or in his home. Nevertheless, a concerted effort was made to locate her at the residence.

On the night we executed the search warrant it was late. Detectives had already worked 16-hour shifts and everyone was tired. The decision was made to execute the search warrant, do an initial assessment of the home, make a list of personnel and resources that would be needed the next day, and then send everyone home to get a few hours of sleep before hitting the ground running in the morning.

When I arrived back on the scene early the following morning there was a large crowd gathered near the home. Word spread fast about the serial killer and the victims who were decomposing in his home. As we started organizing for the day I received a phone call from a high-ranking boss in my agency. He called to tell me that he wanted "a good thorough investigation done on this case." (It always amazed me how many bosses gave me that order over the course of my career. What did they think? If they didn't tell me to do a good thorough job on my murder investigation that I was going to settle for doing a poor job? Naturally, we're going to take our time and do our best.) He further informed me that I had an open budget on this case. Whatever I needed in terms of equipment or personnel would be granted. "Just ask for it, and we will send it to you" is the way he put it.

Armed with real funding, this complex case was now made exponentially easier. We assembled a crime scene team of 15 investigators just to work on processing the house—11 would work outside and four inside. Despite a full team and abundant resources, it took 29 days to search and process the serial killer's home. Twenty-nine very long days … usually working 12 hours or more per day.

The exciting part of forensics to most people involves what I refer to as the gizmos and gadgets and things that go beep. That is, the high-tech equipment that people see on TV and wish they could use to solve most cases in society. This equipment is terrific, but it doesn't replace the diligent work of a patient investigator.

The New York State Police is one of the largest police agencies in the country. We had a large annual budget compared to most other police agencies (although it still never seemed to be enough). We had most of the available high-tech equipment at our disposal. However, there is still no better way to search a crime scene than with human eyes and human hands. This work takes great patience. Machines don't know how to move things out of the way, separate blades of grass, read through writings at the scene to see if they might contain probative information. Scientific equipment can identify people, break down substances into their most basic components, and trace artifacts back to their respective sources. That same equipment cannot find the data to analyze, nor can it decide what data is most pertinent to the case. Everything scientific follows a scientific method, and all scientific methods begin with data collection. You can't analyze and opine unless you first have data to analyze. That's where the investigator comes in.

Finding evidence isn't always easy. It takes patience. Especially in this serial killer's home. It would be nice if all crime scene searches took place in a well-kept, clean residence. But that's rare. Most crime scene searches happen in homes that are in some state of disarray. Some much worse than others. Bloodstains are easy to find in a clean, well maintained home. Not so much in a filthy home. The greater the disarray, the greater the challenge.

The team of police personnel involved in a major case investigation goes well beyond the crime scene search. While 15 investigators are searching the residence, many others are providing scene security. Closing roads, escorting neighbors in and out of the street, giving directions to detour around the area, and providing security to the van holding the evidence that has been removed that day. There is as much patience involved in scene security as there is in scene searching. The officer on duty must pay careful attention, remain vigilant on his feet, and not leave his post until officially relieved by competent authority.

The extent to which a residence or building is searched depends upon the facts and circumstances of the case, as well as what is specified within the search warrant. In this case, we were looking for human remains, among other evidence. The missing person whom Ken denied killing, who may or may not be located on the property or in the home, disappeared about 18 months prior. The body would likely be quite decomposed and probably skeletonized.

Locating human remains among clutter and mess in a home takes time in itself, especially locating smaller bones such as fingers, toes, and vertebrae. But disinterring a body that has been buried is a long methodical process. Once the remains are located, they are usually disinterred using hand brooms and garden trowels. Loose dirt is swept away until the broom is no longer effective. Garden trowels are then used to gently scrape away harder soil in order to loosen it up, then the broom sweeps away the loosened soil. This a time-consuming process that requires a great deal of care and patience. Once all the soil has been removed from the remains, the body is very carefully lifted on one side and then the other until a clean white sheet can be maneuvered under the remains. Once the sheet is in place, the victim is removed from the shallow grave and wrapped in the sheet to be transported for autopsy.

Once the three victims were carefully removed from the crawlspace, the five skeletonized victims in the attic were located and removed. This required not only sorting through years of clutter piled up in the attic, but it required pulling apart attic insulation, separating articles of clothing, and sorting through decomposed human tissue.

Once the victims in Ken's home were removed it was time to search for evidence. Every item in the home was carefully moved; examined with human eyes and touched with human hands. No fancy equipment at this point. Just a careful and methodical review of the contents of the home. Each item in the home was reviewed in order to ascertain whether or not it had probative value in the case. Those items deemed probative to the case were documented, recorded, and secured.

During the full 29-day investigation, the exterior and the interior of Ken's home was thoroughly searched. Grid searches were performed on the exterior of the home. Investigators lined up shoulder to shoulder and literally crawled from the front property line to the rear property line. Anything found located in the yard that is not a rock, stick, leaf, or blade of grass was carefully examined to determine its probable value. After the visual examination of the yard was complete, and appropriate evidence collected, the rear yard was excavated to search below the surface.

Despite the most diligent and patient efforts of investigators, not all questions will be answered in every case. Budding investigators should be aware that, despite their best efforts, not all cases will be fully solved. In this case, to date, the last victim on the missing person list has not been found. Ken has never been charged or connected to her disappearance. Possibilities abound. The victim whom Ken did not admit to killing went missing prior to the family building a new garage on the property. What better place to hide a murder victim than under a poured concrete floor? Investigators directed this area to be checked. The concrete floor of the garage was removed and its underlying areas searched. This entailed renting jack hammers to remove the concrete and manually digging below the surface in an effort to locate the body.

After an extensive and exhaustive 29-day crime scene investigation, a final review of the scene was conducted prior to the home being released. The investigation, however, continued until Ken entered a guilty plea about two years after his arrest. He was sentenced to eight consecutive life sentences without the possibility of parole.

Conclusion

The job of a crime scene investigator is complex and difficult yet fulfilling. The patient investigator is rewarded with a sense of satisfaction in a job well done, regardless of the actual outcome. I never thought of the job of an investigator as being one that "puts bad guys in jail" or "achieves justice for victims." However, there is a satisfaction with figuring something out. The investigator is a fact finder. He or she separates fact from fiction. The investigator separates what is *possible* from what is *probable*. He or she categorizes probative/actual/supportable evidence from hollow claims and assumptions. The investigator finds physical evidence that either corroborates or refutes spoken words; constantly re-assessing new theories against case evidence.

An investigator must be objective and open minded. He or she doesn't arrive at a conclusion, and then make the evidence fit. He or she follows the evidence where it leads.

An investigator must separate compassion from emotion. It's not wrong to feel compassion for a fellow human being, but emotion may cause an investigator to lose objectivity. Emotions must be left at home. I've been accused of being "desensitized" to death and tragedy. I never saw it that way. It's simply a matter of leaving emotions out of it. You have a job to do, and you must stay objective in doing it.

It's also important to understand that a police investigator actually has a duty that is twofold. You have an obligation to find facts that eventually will be used in the prosecution of a criminal defendant. But at the same time, you have an obligation to protect the fundamental due process rights to which that defendant is entitled. This comes back to objectivity and impartiality. Fact finding. Finding, assessing, and following the evidence where it leads you. It will eventually take shape. The truth will be told. It just takes a great deal of patience.

Note

1. *Oxford Living Dictionary.*

Chapter 5

Energy

Matthew Spaier

Congratulations, you want to be an investigator … but where do you start? This is an important question that many people ask when they want to get into this business. In my opinion, the number one key to success in this profession is "energy." Merriam-Webster defines energy as "the vigorous exertion of power: effort." Future investigators can harness this energy to be successful. I know from experience. I started my own private investigation firm in 2005.

In this chapter, I will walk you through my personal journey. My story will illustrate the energy needed to establish a new career as an investigator, run a Private Investigation business, and to have an inventory of successful cases.

There is a tremendous amount of energy involved in investigative work. It is the job of the investigator to determine the "who, what, when, where and how." Energetic investigators will always have an advantage in this business. There is a lot of work involved with investigations. It is important to understand that as an investigator, your research process will never be "finished." You are never done learning your craft.

The best investigators use their energy wisely, following proper techniques and procedures. While no investigator can guarantee a certain result, a good investigator will always guarantee that they used good judgment and exhausted all available leads and resources. You must be willing to put in the work.

Learning how to become a PI will require a lot of energy. Knowing where to start is essential to success. There isn't a straightforward process to becoming a private investigator, there are not many resources available, and handbooks on how to get started in this business are few and far between. It is also difficult to find a mentor.

The laws and procedure for becoming a PI vary by state. My business is in New York. Here, if you do not have a law enforcement background, you need a PI mentor to become a licensed private investigator. The New York State Division of Licensing also requires you to pass a Private Investigator test to operate in New York. You also must follow General Business law (see NY Gen Bus L §71 (2012)).

Before you can take the Private Investigator license test, you need to have three years working experience in the field or have a law enforcement background.

My story starts in the Spring of 1996. Then, I had the honor of walking down the aisle at the Paramount Theater (Madison Square Garden) as part of the graduating class of John Jay College of Criminal Justice. At John Jay, I received a Bachelor's of Science in Criminal Justice with a minor in Police Science. To gain experience, I performed three separate internships with the New York City Department of Investigations (NYC DOI). NYC DOI is one of the oldest law enforcement agencies in the country. It operates as an internal watchdog for its City's employees and contractors.

It takes a lot of energy to participate in three unpaid internships while attending school. I knew that putting in the extra effort to do the internships would provide amazing opportunities to learn from some of the best investigators in New York City. I was surprised to learn that few college students participate in internship programs. Having the drive to take the extra time to balance studies with work experience is a must when getting into this industry. Experience will always give you an advantage.

Despite my internship experience, getting permanent work as an investigator was challenging. NYC instituted a three-year hiring freeze in 1995 that prevented my permanent hire at NYC DOI or any other City agency. I was forced to look for any opportunity that presented itself. I began searching classified ads and checking for available police tests. I took several tests and scored well. I also applied to other investigative positions. However, for one reason or another, I was not getting any real opportunities.

Finally, I found a solid lead. It was a job posting for a retail investigation company that was looking for reference checkers. I was interviewed and hired on the spot at a pay rate of $6.00 an hour. Within two hours of working on my first day, I was promoted to Field Investigator. This was an excellent opportunity. The company had a strong Mystery Shopping division and this promotion would have me doing field work. Within six months of my hire, my supervisor left his position and I was promoted to Director of Operations. I was given a salary of $35,000 a year and a company car. I remained with this company until 1998. While there, I learned how to interview potential employees and became an expert in doing background checks and verifications. I had no idea how valuable these skills would be in the future.

After I left that position, I decided to leverage my investigative experience in the human resources field by becoming a recruiter. I worked my way up through the company to become the manager of the technical recruiter division. As a recruiter, I kept my investigative skills sharp by verifying the resumes of the IT professionals I was trying to place. I remained with this company until August 27, 2001. I had a job interview scheduled on September 11, 2001 across the street from the former World Trade Center. On September 7, they called me and rescheduled the interview to September 12. The job interview unfortunately never happened. Although I didn't realize it at the time, I was about to return to the investigative field.

A few weeks later, I had a discussion with a personal injury attorney in the Bronx. He offered me a position as his "in-house" investigator. I took him up on the offer and called my former supervisor at the mystery shopping company. He had started a Private Investigation company and had been in business for several years. He agreed to mentor me and helped me learn the role of a private investigator in a personal injury case. From that experience, I learned the importance of finding a mentor in this business. We remain close to this day and often bounce ideas off one another. I remained at the law firm until September 1, 2005.

About six months before leaving the law firm, I had a decision to make. The lawyer I worked for was encouraging me to also become a lawyer. I considered it, but always felt strongly that I wanted to be a Private Investigator and start my own business. While working for the attorney, I passed the test to become a licensed Private Investigator and I have held that license since 2003. I also became a Notary Public during that time. I have since learned that having a Notary Public License is an essential credential for any private investigator. You will be required to notarize statements and affidavits.

Finally, my dream of being a business owner became a reality. In June of 2005, I incorporated Satellite Investigations and transferred my personal PI license into a business PI license. This would allow me to expand my business, by hiring employees. I began to research how to fund my business. I ended up going to the bank, where I secured a small business loan for $35,000. The attorney I worked for agreed to be my first client and I was able to get several more clients through networking.

On September 1, 2005 I officially opened my business to the public. I had a physical office, I made business cards and I created a website. Very early on I had the vision to specialize in the type of personal injury investigative work that I had already been doing. It came naturally, because of my prior experience.

It took a tremendous amount of energy to build my business. When I first opened, I had very little work. I needed to get clients and start building my business. I refused to waste any time. I started from scratch and decided to find some clients, so I picked up the phone book and began cold calling every law firm that was listed. I called, introduced myself, and tried to sell my services. I offered special incentives for new clients and gave credits for any referrals. I also put a lot of energy into networking and building my professional circle. Through networking, I met a photography expert that gave me overflow work and referred clients to me. All of these efforts involved hard work and required putting in lots of hours. It ended up being worth every second that it took. My only regret during this time was overpaying myself as the "President" of the company. I probably should have taken less money out of my business, and instead, used the funds to grow it further.

By January of 2006, I had a small business, but it was not growing at the pace I hoped for. My bank account had dwindled down to my last $5000. I used this opportunity to push hard and further market myself. I was also blessed with several clients that had multiple assignments and paid their bills very quickly. By June of 2006, I started to get a hold in my little niche. By this time, word of mouth started spreading from my clients and I began to get good paying accounts. I also found a second mentor at this point. He was an attorney that was my third client. He took the time to correct my mistakes and showed me how to do my job better. Over the years, he referred me to many clients and helped me become a better investigator.

My efforts started paying off. In September of 2006, I hired my first employee. I learned that surrounding yourself with good people who want to work is key to a small business. I also learned that knowing when to delegate work or administrative tasks to an employee is key to growth.

Today, our business model has not changed, but our approach has evolved. I coined the tag line "Get results, not excuses" very early on. I found that most of the accounts that I took over were from investigators that were not very good and grossly overcharged and underperformed for their clients.

When using energy, it is important to be efficient. I learned that it was "better to know an expert than be an expert." Rather than using energy to try to accomplish a task that I do not specialize in, I can be more efficient by engaging specialists. Although we specialize in Plaintiff personal injury investigations, we also have a huge network of other investigators that specialize in other areas, such as surveillance, process service and due diligence. By focusing our energy and resources into a specific sub-category of our industry, we are able to offer a top notch service to our clients. Having relationships with "experts" you can count on makes your client happy and makes you look good.

Although I found success, the work never ends. I am always putting energy into growing my business. In 2007, I made the effort to join trade associations and marketing groups. I joined every group I could find and continued to network. This meant attending many events in the evenings after my regular business hours. Overall, it required a lot of my time and energy. The benefit to this was spending time and building relationships with clients. I have always counted on my clients to be an extended sales team to recommend our service. My method works. We currently work with about 80 law firms a year. Most are repeat clients. I have always kept my pricing fair and it has always led to repeat business.

As my experience advanced, I was able to raise my rate. My expertise and the cost of running a business in New York has always helped to drive that number up. I have always understood how to connect with my clients: understand their needs, and give them exactly what they want in a timely fashion. I am also constantly learning and growing, in order to advance my business, to offer more services, and to employ the latest investigative techniques.

As a new investigator, it is important to remember to put your energy into your business. Over time, you will constantly grow and advance your skills. Remember that, in the beginning, you will not know how to do everything. You will always learn on the job how to do your work better. A good investigator will invest each piece of knowledge into their next assignment. This is a building block industry. You are constantly learning how to do your job more efficiently and how to get better results. A good investigator will retain these lessons and foster their relationships.

In 2017, true to my words, I advanced my business by venturing into emerging technology. The investigative industry is constantly changing. The implementation of technology has caused a boom in the ability of the PI to gain information for their cases. I identified Social Media and the research behind it as an avenue to capitalize on. The result has really set my business ahead of the competition. This was a journey that required time and energy. I learned a lot during this process. Technology can be expensive. It is important to really understand your industry and only buy what is needed.

My strategy was as follows. First, I identified several businesses that I thought could help me offer a top-rated product. I began to formulate a marketing strategy. Every successful investigation turned into a case study that I could communicate to demonstrate the value of my new services. With the use of constant contact or another mass email program, I could get the word out about my services and the successful results obtained.

I also put more efforts into positioning myself as an industry leader. I joined several well-known Investigator groups that advocate for the rights of Private Investigators. I also began lending my expertise by serving on the board of directors on these organizations. I have served on the Board of the Associated Licensed Detectives of New York State since 2009. I currently hold the title of Second Vice President. I'm also very involved with the National Council of Investigators and Security Services. Both organizations advocate and lobby for our industry. My involvement with these organizations resulted in several marketing and speaking events. I have had the privilege to lecture at my alma mater, John Jay College of Criminal Justice, and I have written articles for *PI Magazine* and the New York State Trial Lawyers Association. I was also asked to teach a continuing education lecture to personal injury lawyers in 2018.

Ultimately, my energy, drive and passion for what I do has taken me to levels in my business that I could only have dreamed of. My story is not finished and continues to grow daily.

The next portion of this chapter will provide you with some case studies that demonstrate the value of hard work. They further illustrate the winning investigative combination of technology, networking and "old fashioned" detective work. I am most proud of my ability to help the people who have hired my clients to represent them.

Case Study #1: The Broken Fire Escape

In February 2018 at approximately 7pm, I received a phone call from a client. He had a meeting scheduled the following day with the family of a woman who had been in a serious accident earlier that month. My client was going to be pitching his law firm and wanted some "Ammunition" to bring with him to the meeting. He asked me to pull up any information I could on the accident and find witnesses.

His meeting was at 11am the following morning. Time was of the essence. It was clear that energy was needed to really dig into this case in such a short time frame. However, this is quite typical. As a PI, you must be accessible at all times and be willing to work very strange and often long hours.

The timing of this case was very good, in terms of my ability to add value. Several months earlier, I had started to develop a relationship with a company that offered Social Media research through Geo-tagging and Geo-fencing. Geo-tagging adds geographical information to metadata, such as a videos, photos or tweets. Geo-fencing is location-based searching. Due to the nature of this accident, the case was the perfect candidate for this new technology.

Here are the facts. We knew that on the day of the accident, two people had been walking on the sidewalk in front of a building in downtown New York City. We also knew that a building inspection was taking place at the same exact time. An inspector was on the seventh floor of the building on the fire escape when a 150-pound steel piece broke off. The piece struck and killed one of the pedestrians and seriously injured a female pedestrian, who sustained a brain injury. My client was going to meet with the injured person and her family. My client had no information other than then name of her brother, who had called him and provided the room number at the hospital. It took me about 30 minutes to locate the woman who was injured and pull her pedigree, or background information. Within the hour, I had set up a Geo-fence and keyword search.

While that was happening, I decided to do some Open Source Investigations. This is a fancy term for "Searching the Net." I found many useful news articles on the incident. I also decided to do some research on the building itself and found that there were some prior violations regarding the fire escape and the fire alarm system. I also determined that that the building was 17 days overdue on its fire escape inspection. Building code requires this to be done every five years and they had missed the deadline by 17 days. I also pulled the actual administrative code for my client to review.

After taking a brief dinner break, I returned to check on the data that was pulled from the Geo-tag/Keyword search. I found over 10,000 posts on social media during the time of the accident spanning a two-hour window. Using investigative techniques, I was able to narrow the search to 300 people either posting or reposting about the accident. I found eight direct eyewitnesses. Several had photos and video of the area and incident just after the accident happened.

Due to my efforts, my client now had considerably more evidence to support his claim for compensation. Energy, drive and due diligence certainly played a part in resolving this matter. I worked well into the evening to get these results for my client. Having the necessary energy, along with the tools to get the job done helped provide a positive result.

It is important to note that the Geo-tagging and Keyword search technology I utilized was introduced to me by someone in my personal network. This illustrates the value of networking in the investigative field.

Case Study #2: Open Data Research and the 311 NYC Complaint Database

The next case study also demonstrates the value of energy combined with networking. In this instance, I utilized a new investigative tool leveraging Open Data research. I was also introduced to this technology from someone in my network.

In 2018, I attended a seminar given by the New York Chapter of the Association of Certified Fraud Examiners. This is another professional organization I joined in order to advance my network. The speaker was a computer programmer who works for an investigation company that specializes in Due Diligence screenings. Due Diligence Screening is a type of background check.

After the class, I spoke with a programmer and we agreed to meet up to discuss the New York City 311 Open Data system. New York City has made almost 20 million records available online regarding prior complaints to City agencies, involving anything from noise complaints to broken sidewalks. I decided this data could be useful in my investigations. The end result of our collaboration is a unique research product that searches the system for specific complaints at addresses, geo-locations and also by agency for prior complaints about defective conditions.

This is a new type of research. The city had always made the data available, but they send it to you in huge "data sets" with no way to analyze the data. Our program does all the leg work to analyze the data sets. These types of searches have been game changers for the investigative industry. Now when a Freedom of Information Law (FOIL) request is entered, a unique ID is provided and the FOIL clerk must send the requested records.

This search proved to be critical in a recent case in Staten Island. A defective condition existed on a particular road. It had actually been incorrectly identified in the initial filing as being in the southwest corner of the intersection. The defect was actually in the northeast corner. I discovered this error because of the investigative tool that I developed. Our search used Geo-location coordinates to identify the correct area and pulled the necessary records. The records showed not only that the condition had existed, but it had previously been repaired insufficiently about three months prior to my client's accident.

The value of using my energy to network, created the opportunity to provide an innovative search product that is only available through my business.

Case Study #3: Tree on the Belt Parkway

The next case also demonstrates the incredible energy required to solve a case. This case involves an accident that happened in June 2018 on a roadway in Brooklyn, NY. A man had finished work and was heading home on the Belt Parkway at about 8 am. Suddenly a tree crashed through his windshield and severed three of his fingers. The tree branch also impaled the driver. He continued to drive a quarter mile before coming to a stop. The driver lost several vital organs but miraculously survived the accident.

There happened to be a substantial number of eyewitnesses to this incident. Several of them happened to use a smartphone app called Citizen. Citizen allows a person who signs up to essentially become a reporter. The person receives an alert and is encouraged to record and report about the alert in the network.

This resource was very helpful in identifying the exact location of the incident. The City had dispatched the Parks and Recreation Department to remove all dead trees on the roadway and this made it almost impossible to locate the exact tree stump involved in the accident. Using case file photos and the Citizen app video, I was able to locate the exact area where the tree fell. Once out on the scene, I found the remains of the tree and was able to preserve it for further testing. Open Source research suggested the trees had been dead since Hurricane Sandy flooded the area in 2012. This was confirmed by the research where 27 prior complaints about the dangers of the dead trees on this roadway were in the system. This information will again be helpful in obtaining an early resolution for the injured person. We were also able to track down and interview 12 direct eyewitnesses.

Case Study #4: Motorcycle Accident in the Bronx

In this case, a tremendous amount of energy was utilized to interview witnesses located on social media. In February 2017, a man was riding his motorcycle on a roadway in the Bronx, NY. He was involved in an accident with two tractor trailer trucks, one of which fled the scene of the accident. This man had very serious injuries and I was contacted by his attorney to gather information on the case. A site investigation and an onsite canvass was done with very few results obtained.

However, through Geotag/Keyword searching, we located several eyewitnesses that told a very different story. These people were located through Twitter. We were able to make contact and they agreed to be interviewed. They actually put the blame on the motorcyclist due to his reckless riding. This was something that was not favorable to the client. We were also able to learn that the rider simply lost control and hit one of the tractor trailers. The contact was the direct result of the motorcyclist's negligence.

Upon review of the facts, my client decided to drop the case. My firm was contacted by three other law firms after the case was dropped for a liability analysis. Because the injuries were so severe, the injured person was still trying to find an attorney to take his case. Here, the truth was uncovered very early on. This was helpful to my client because they did not have to invest time and resources into a case that would probably be lost during discovery. My client gladly paid his bill to be able to tell the client that he did not have a case.

Conclusion

The common theme in this chapter is energy. As this chapter has demonstrated, energy is important to our investigations. As investigators, we expend great amounts of energy in opening and maintaining our successful businesses. We also energetically use all avenues available to complete an investigation. In my business, we have relied on accident site investigations, conventional canvassing, electronic canvassing, Open Source Investigations, open data research and witness research.

The key to being a successful investigator today is to have the ability to combine traditional investigative methods with emerging technology. The ability to succeed as a small operation is dependent on your ability to incorporate technology and to have a good work ethic. In this industry, you learn on the job and often learn how to do something new while you are investigating an existing case. Take memos and open a "how to" file. This will help you in the future for your next case.

"Energy," "Drive," or "Due Diligence" is a must for any start up business no matter what the field. It is not limited to business owners only. At any level of investigation, full effort is required for the best results. You must be able to chase down leads. You must be able to consider alternate possibilities. Like any good scientist, you must test scientific method and prove or discount theories. As an investigator, this technique just happens to take place in real life events and not by hypothesis. This is especially important when you have to testify about your findings. You may need to lay a good foundation as to how you developed an opinion or fact pattern. Stick to the truth, keep good notes and always be prepared for questions on the stand to try and throw you off. Over the years I have been asked many questions unrelated to my investigation in depositions and while on the stand. It is common practice.

The opportunities for success in this industry are limitless. It is a good strategy to find a niche and be the expert of a certain type of investigation. I have used every job experience and essentially every case experience to build on the next job or assignment. The energy I put forth since the very beginning of my career has helped me to push cases forward and has opened countless doors from an investigative and marketing perspective.

In closing, find your passion, don't be afraid to fail and put your best effort forward. Build on each success and don't be embarrassed to get the word out. Having the right energy, drive and knowledge takes time. Don't be discouraged. In the end you will always reap what you sow in this industry. Find a mentor and always try to improve your skill-set through experience or by educational webinars. You will be amazed at the level of your success if you stay focused and work every lead in your case.

Chapter 6

Initiative

Daniel R. Alonso

The ability to show initiative separates average, or even good, investigators from their more successful colleagues. Whether an investigator is in a detective squad, FBI office, prosecutor's office, private investigative firm, or corporate setting, it is always easier for him or her to sit at a desk and wait for the phone to ring or for a supervisor to walk by with an assignment. Even when a case is already on the investigator's plate, an investigation turns into nothing more than a "check-the-box" exercise, where the investigator simply goes from Point A to Point B by interviewing the expected witnesses and reviewing the expected documents. The result of such an investigation goes something like this: "Witness A said this, Witness B said that, the documents showed some things and not others, and we were able to draw some conclusions but not others due to insufficient evidence."

That is not what truly effective investigators do.

To be at the top of your game as an investigator requires initiative, the focus of this chapter. What does that mean? In the first place, it's the opposite of sitting at your desk. It means constantly looking for the investigative lead that turns into a great matter, and it means developing a sixth sense that tells you when pulling a thread will unravel a whole scheme. It's the difference between the investigator who reads the four corners of a fraud file and solves the one allegation involving one victim, versus the investigator who asks, "How many other times did this guy do this?"

Initiative does not necessarily come easily to everyone, nor was it a quality I particularly possessed when I began my career as an investigative prosecutor at the Manhattan DA's office in 1991. However, in those early years, I learned from a series of lawyers senior to me[1] that, in investigations, sitting back is not an option. If you have some witnesses but not enough, try to use one to secretly record the subject of the investigation. If you have evidence of one payoff in an ongoing scheme, apply for a wiretap to prove the broader scheme and gather evidence against everyone responsible. And always—always—take advantage of an opportunity to speak to the perpetrator. Not only do you have a chance to gain valuable admissions, but you might learn something or "flip" him against others. In other words, show *initiative*.

Seventeen years later, I took those lessons with me and used them in the case discussed in the next section.

Case Study in Initiative

In February of 2008, during a hot South American summer, I found myself at a table outside a small café in one of the *barrios* of the Autonomous City of Buenos Aires, Argentina. Earlier that day, I had been directed to sit down when I arrived, put my travel cellphone on the table, and await a call with further instructions. After a few excruciating minutes, during which I wondered if I was crazy to have accepted this invitation, the phone rang. The man who had arranged the meeting—a defrauded investor in a $43 million investment fraud scheme—told me, in Spanish, to go inside the café. When I did so, slowly and with trepidation, I found Diego Mariano Rolando—the mastermind of the scheme—waiting to talk with me.

Over the course of the next four hours, over coffee and Argentine pastries, Rolando told me chapter and verse of the fraud that he had perpetrated during the previous three years through a bogus company that he had created, IATrading. As the court-appointed receiver for IATrading, I hung on his every word, and was not surprised by his tale of deception and fraud. What did surprise me was learning that—as Rolando told me and I later corroborated—many of the investors, on whose behalf I was fighting to recover money, had been lying to me. Indeed, they themselves had been committing a fraud against me, the receiver.

How did I come to be in that café in that Buenos Aires *barrio*, and how on earth did I manage to fall victim to fraud myself? For the answer, we have to start at the beginning, long before I ever heard of IATrading.com.

My parents and I immigrated to the United States from Argentina in 1968, when I was not quite three years old. My earliest memory in this country is of my first day of nursery school, when I thought to myself (in a Spanish, three-year-old version), "Holy Cow. I don't speak these people's language!" Thanks to the infant brain, that soon changed, but I was extremely fortunate to maintain my Spanish throughout my life. In contrast to many Argentine families then in the U.S., where the parents purposely did not speak Spanish at home so they could practice their English with the kids (who rarely learned Spanish well), my family continued to speak Spanish at home. As a result, I never lost my fluency.

Fast forward more than 20 years later, when, as a third-year student at NYU School of Law, I found a flyer in my mailbox at the law school. "Spanish-language interpreters and translators needed, NYU Law Clinics—$12.50 per hour." Focusing primarily on the amount they were offering (a fortune to me back then), I said to myself, "Sure—I can do this." Unfortunately, I only spoke "home/family Spanish," having never studied the language or taken a class that was taught in

Spanish. So, like a good budding lawyer, after persuading the clinic leadership that, no problem, I was qualified to translate legal documents and carry out simultaneous interpretation, I ran to the library and found the best Spanish–English dictionary and legal Spanish phrasebook I could find.

After three days of intensive study, I had upped my fluency to include legal Spanish, with some business Spanish thrown in. Aside from being well-paid (by 1989 student standards) for my efforts, the learning experience left me ready to tackle any Spanish-language assignment. And I was able to burnish those skills further when I became an Assistant District Attorney and, later, an Assistant U.S. Attorney. I did so not by involving myself in Spanish-language cases—as an American prosecutor who hailed from South America, I studiously avoided being pigeonholed—but by volunteering when the offices' public relations people needed someone to go on Spanish-language radio or television.

Media appearances were of course a small part of what I did as a prosecutor. I focused enormous effort on honing my investigative skills, and became particularly enamored of using grand juries for investigative purposes, as well as electronic eavesdropping in long-term investigations. Over the years, I investigated or supervised many fascinating fraud and corruption cases, including prosecuting the first trial in the famous "Wolf of Wall Street" case involving the securities fraud boiler room, Stratton Oakmont, and the notorious fraudster, Jordan Belfort. I also prosecuted or oversaw many other cases, including against corrupt elected officials and police officers, corporate fraud at public companies, the then-largest staged car accident scheme prosecuted in New York history, labor racketeering and construction fraud schemes throughout the city, and a private-sector corruption case in which dozens of lawyers were indicted for a kickback scheme and fraud. I also negotiated corporate settlement agreements with the Bank of New York and the New York Racing Association, among others, and argued the appeal of the seminal Second Circuit case on honest services mail fraud.

To be sure, all those cases involved initiative, on my part and that of the agents and police officers with whom I teamed up, and one could argue that a good number of them were more significant in the vast world of fraud than the Rolando investment scam. But as we will see, none tested my initiative and creativity as much, and few were as fun.

Having amassed experience as both a state and a federal prosecutor, and having appeared repeatedly on Spanish media, I was, by the time I left the U.S. Attorney's Office for private practice in 2005, ready to conduct business in Spanish-speaking countries. I entered the private practice of law interested in conducting internal investigations for public and private companies, representing executives in criminal and other enforcement investigations, and, hopefully, securing an appointment as a monitor or similar third-party role. In my first couple of years at Kaye Scholer, I conducted a good number of investigations, cut my teeth for the first time in my career in civil litigation, and was appointed by the Governor of New York to serve on the Commission on Public Integrity. But I had not gotten that elusive third-party assignment.

That's where things stood when I got a call in early 2008 from Jo Mettenburg, a smart and enthusiastic Trial Lawyer in the Kansas City office of the Commodity Futures Trading Commission. My friends in the New York office—lawyers I had met while in law school, some of whom remained my mentors throughout my career[2]—had recommended that she call to explore whether I was available to be a receiver in a fraud case that she was about to file. Having previously sought, without success, court-appointed monitorships, I was eager for an independent, third-party assignment within my area of expertise, which was complex investigations of fraud and corruption.

Bingo. Jo and her partner, Ken McCracken, had been investigating a somewhat messy investment fraud scheme with some aspects of a Ponzi scheme, in which 90 percent of the investors in the $43 million scheme, as well as the scheme's mastermind, were located in Argentina. I knew about Ponzi schemes from my years as a prosecutor, and had prosecuted or supervised their prosecution on a number of occasions. Although this one was not nearly as big as the Bernard Madoff scheme that was unfolding at the same time, it involved a large amount of money, and many victims were out their life savings. Jo said that she was interested in my serving as the receiver because of my background investigating white-collar crime and because of my Spanish skills. I jumped at the chance, and told Jo that I was eager to help. I knew then that my familiarity with the culture of Argentina would come in handy in the assignment as well.

The work began immediately after United States District Judge Mark Kravitz, to whom the CFTC case had been assigned, formally appointed me the receiver for the assets of Diego Mariano Rolando, aka Roclerman, aka ROC, doing business as (d/b/a) IATrading.com. Receivers are like bankruptcy trustees, but in a context other than a bankruptcy proceeding. The receiver's job is to step into the legal shoes of the person or entity at issue, with all the powers and duties that such person or entity has, including disposing of the assets of the estate. Some receiverships involve purely administrative work, such as taking over a forfeited art gallery, selling the paintings, and distributing the proceeds to the appropriate parties. But others, like this one, involve an investigative component that is like catnip to those of us who investigate fraud for a living. Either way, the goal is to recover as many assets as possible as quickly as possible, and present a reasonable plan to the court for the distribution of those assets to creditors. In this case, the looming questions were (1) how much of Rolando's money could we find, and (2) what was the fairest way to return that money to the investors, understanding that we would never be able to return all monies.

I attacked the assignment with gusto, enlisting my law firm (Kaye Scholer) and a retired FBI agent, Dan Gill, to assist me with the investigation. We took control of the accounts we knew about in the U.S., disabled and forensically preserved his website, spent some time with the CFTC getting up to speed, and began the arduous task of communicating with investors. We quickly learned how the basic scheme worked, but to figure out where in the world the assets might be, we needed to understand the fraud. As a prosecutor, I always found that my teams and I could better decipher the contours of a fraudulent scheme if we understood the perpetrator—who he was and what motivated him. And of course, the goal always was to interview the perpetrator/defendant, usually as a last step in a meticulously prepared case. It helped to learn more about the case as I sought to talk to Rolando himself. I had to *know* Rolando before I spoke to him—and learned a lot in short order.

In 2000, Diego Mariano Rolando, then in his early 20s, won a contest sponsored by a leading Argentine financial newspaper, *Ámbito Financiero*. In the contest, "Ámbito del Millón," contestants "invested" a hypothetical amount of money, with the person who achieved the highest percentage being declared the winner. Rolando entered the contest twice: once under his own name and once under a pseudonym/ nickname, "Roclerman." The Roclerman entry won the contest by a significant margin. As a result of the contest, he had gained fame and notoriety in Argentina, and a reputation as a shrewd investor. In the early 2000s, friends and acquaintances began to invest through Rolando, who would in turn trade the investors' money (at first legitimately, as in many investment schemes) in brokerage accounts in his own name.

As the number of investors grew, Rolando started a website, IATrading.com, to solicit investments and allow new investors real-time access to their account information. The "IA" stood for Interactive Brokers, a legitimate broker-dealer located in Connecticut, through which Rolando effected trades with the investors' money. Rolando falsely represented to his investors that IATrading.com was an affiliate of Interactive Brokers, when in reality it was simply a website run by Rolando and his sister out of their Buenos Aires apartment. He did not mention to his investors that he ran the website. Emails sent to the "customer service" address on the website would be answered by Rolando himself, and the listed toll-free number went to a third-party service in the U.S.

The fake company and website were just the initial lies Rolando told his victims. His primary misrepresentations involved the nature of the investments. Personally and through a network of brokers that Rolando recruited, he persuaded clients to invest with him by touting his success in the *Ámbito del Millón* contest and persuading them that he had devised an investment system focused on conservative growth through investments in highly rated stocks in U.S. markets. He specifically told investors that trading would take place exclusively on the New York Stock Exchange or through the NASDAQ system, and that trading would be done only in blue chip stocks and high-grade index funds. He promised them an attractive, but in the scheme of things modest, return of 1–2 percent per month. Rolando also claimed that he only did day trading, so that accounts would be fully liquid at the end of each day.

Based on these representations, Rolando lured nearly 400 investors to invest more than $43 million. As astute readers will have figured out by now, these representations were mostly false. He was investing their money, to be sure, but

95 percent of his investment activity involved risky and speculative trades in commodity futures and options on commodity futures. As anyone with a passing knowledge of trading knows, complex derivative products such as futures and options have a potentially enormous upside, but they are also a great way to lose everything. It's hard for most people (I am no exception!) even to get their heads around calculating the value of an option to buy or sell a futures contract, the value of which itself is derivative of the underlying commodity. But in the heady days of 2005 through 2007, Rolando did just that, and was able to deliver the conservative returns he had promised his investors, while making much more for himself on his derivatives trading. In other words, he thought he could make his investors money while making himself a lot more—but putting only *their* money at risk.

"You only find out who is swimming naked when the tide goes out," Warren Buffett famously said. It was no different with Rolando: while the market was booming, his scheme worked. Indeed, Rolando was so reliable that many of his clients used IATrading.com essentially as a virtual bank, visiting Rolando personally to make cash deposits and withdrawals. This may seem odd to people from countries with reliable banking systems, but Argentines at that time trusted neither their government nor their financial system. Seven years earlier, the government had notoriously and by fiat converted all dollar-denominated accounts into peso accounts, wiping out 2/3 of the wealth of its citizens overnight. On top of that, currency controls later imposed by the left-wing government that was operating during Rolando's scheme meant that it was difficult for Argentines to maintain dollar accounts within Argentina any longer. Operating outside the banking system, or any regulation, Rolando was able to give his clients what the Argentine banking system could not.

But once the market started crashing just before the recession of 2008, Rolando's losses began to mount. As a result, in a Ponzi-type pattern, he began to use the assets of some investors to fund the redemption requests by others. Unfortunately, as the crisis worsened, investors clamored for redemptions that exceeded Rolando's ability to pay them. That, in turn, prompted some investors to contact Interactive Brokers, which led that American brokerage to freeze Rolando's access to what was left in the accounts he controlled. And then the CFTC stepped in. Jo Mettenburg recommended me to Judge Kravitz to seize the assets and investigate, and we were off to the races.

As the receiver, my main job other than the investigation and recovery of assets was to devise a fair plan by which to return recovered assets to the investors. I quickly put together a team, and chose as my right-hand professional Keith Murphy, a senior bankruptcy associate who had worked on SEC receiverships in the past, and who would later spend years working on the Madoff case under the trustee appointed by the Securities Investor Protection Corporation. The initial steps were easy: Keith and I took control of the IATrading.com website and all of the accounts held at Interactive Brokers. We set up a website of my own with which to communicate with investors, and issued restraining notices to a few large banks in case assets were held there. I also sent an email to Diego Rolando's last known email address, more as a "Hail Mary" pass than anything else, as I considered it unlikely that the South American perpetrator of a multi-million dollar fraud would be eager to speak with an investigator appointed by an American court. And I was right: my response was crickets.

In addition to communicating with the investors to tell them generally what my team and I were doing, we needed information *from* the investors as well. Because Rolando ran his scheme partially through real accounts at Interactive Brokers and partly through cash transactions and withdrawals, we had no reliable record of how much investors had put in and how much they took out. We later learned that the IATrading.com website run by Rolando in Argentina—to which all investors had access—was an accurate accounting of money in and money out, but in those early days it was part of our job to find out what was and was not reliable information. To that end, our next step was to send questionnaires to every one of the nearly 400 investors, seeking basic information such as evidence and amounts of their deposits and withdrawals—particularly those made in cash—and any improper transactions reflected in the accounts held at Interactive Brokers. We also needed to confirm their identities, know whether they had invested through Rolando or his brokers, and, importantly, find out what communications they had had with Rolando, and when.

As we began to analyze these questionnaires, it was clear that the scheme was fairly well-organized, with most investors having been sold the same nonsense about safe investments held at an American institution insured by Lloyds of London. Some invested through brokers and some didn't, and a good number said they had made cash deposits and withdrawals before the scheme unraveled. And it also became clear that because of the promised steady 1–2 percent returns, and monthly IATrading statements that reflected those returns, the investors thought they had a lot more money than they had invested, or that was actually left in the accounts. In other words, our review of the questionnaires shed some light on the scheme, but were not in any way surprising.

Allow me to pause the story for a minute to return to our theme of initiative. The receivership estate did not have unlimited means to fund our investigation, and the reality was that every dollar we spent meant that a dollar less would ultimately go to the investors. As a result, it would not have been wrong for us to stop after reviewing the questionnaires and trading records, report to Judge Kravitz what we had found, and return whatever assets we had recovered to the investors, in a pro-rated amount, depending on the amount of their net investments.[3] (We would, of course, give no credit for the fictitious profits that Rolando had both promised the investors and falsely showed on their statements.) Had we stopped and prepared a distribution plan, the investors would have received money from the estate based on what they wrote in their questionnaires. And I would have never learned that a sizeable chunk of investors had lied to me.

But that's not what we did. Something gnawed at me. I couldn't be clear in my own mind whether it was the fact that the investors, obliged by the perpetrators, were using an apartment in Buenos Aires as a bank; that there was a sizeable amount of cash involved; or that an investment fraudster had recruited brokers who were themselves investors. My team and I knew, however, that we couldn't end the investigation there. So I took the initiative and contacted the CFTC to say that I was planning a trip to Argentina, and wanted to make sure the staff did not object to using receivership funds for this purpose. I told them that I wanted to meet with all the investors as a group so that they would have confidence in the receivership and the American legal proceedings, and to answer any questions they had. I also wanted to interview some of the investors in person, and as many of the brokers as possible, to look them in the eye and make sure I wasn't missing anything. Taking this trip was the first of two key moments of initiative in the investigation.

The CFTC did not object, so I recruited a Spanish-speaking associate, Erica Gersowitz (now Erica Bond), to travel with me to Argentina to help me conduct the interviews. Erica's mother was from Colombia, and Erica had grown up speaking Spanish with her grandmother, as I had with mine. As was the case with me before my interpreting job at NYU, she only spoke "home/family" Spanish and had never studied it. I gave her a legal Spanish phrasebook, asked her to study it, and said I had faith that she would do great (I was right). Because every dollar we spent was a dollar less for the investor pool, we had to be frugal. We begged a prominent Argentine law firm, Marval, O'Farrell & Mairal, to lend us a conference room for a week, got an investor who owned a local hotel to host the meeting in his ballroom, and booked our tickets—coach.

We flew overnight to Buenos Aires, arriving the day of our scheduled 10am meeting with the investors. Before we left, I sent another email to Rolando's address, as well as one to his sister, to the effect of, "I am on my way to Buenos Aires to meet with the investors, and was hoping to have the opportunity to meet with you." Maybe Erica didn't think I was necessarily crazy, but she was surely skeptical that someone who was essentially a criminal (though uncharged) would respond positively to such an email, or even respond at all.

Bleary eyed, Erica and I arrived at Buenos Aires's Ezeiza airport and took a car service to the downtown Sheraton. We had barely enough time to shower and change before the hotel owner/investor came to pick us up to drive us to the big meeting. I was a bit nervous. Even though I had been on Spanish-language television, broadcast internationally, I had never before spoken in person to a large group in Spanish, which had not been my native language since I arrived at nursery school 40 years earlier. And these were not people who came to watch an American lawyer give an interesting talk. On the contrary: they were very unhappy, and wanted to know what I was going to do about their situation.

My goals at the meeting were to reassure the investors as best I could, but also to make sure that I set up interview appointments with all of Rolando's brokers/middlemen so that I could continue figuring out exactly how the scam had worked. And my investigative sense told me to be on the lookout for any investors who were not brokers but might nevertheless be interesting to speak with. Never in my most audacious thoughts did I think that one of the investors would lead me to Rolando. But that's exactly what happened.

"Soy el síndico," I told them, using the Spanish word for receiver.

I explained who I was, how I had come to be appointed, and how the receivership worked. I stressed that my team and I were doing our level best to locate and freeze any assets that could be used to compensate them, and asked for any help they could give me in that regard. The principal questions from the investors, not surprisingly, were variations on "How much will we get back?" and "When?" which I tried my best to answer and reassure them as best I could. But the interesting part did not happen until after the meeting was over.

Like students nervously approaching a professor after a lecture, a few of the investors came up to me afterward. In whispered tones, they wanted to know something I hadn't anticipated: was I planning on putting their names and the amounts they had invested in a public report? They seemed very nervous about this fact, which I first chalked up to privacy concerns or embarrassment over having been duped. When I later learned that they had a different reason, I felt silly. Argentines, I knew, were deeply skeptical of their government, and the 2001 peso devaluation had made them more so. As a result, many Argentines invested in physical U.S. currency, or dollar-denominated accounts located "offshore"—which to them often meant Miami. As astute readers will no doubt have figured out, funds held in these ways are not often declared, giving the country an enormous tax evasion problem. My "victims," it seemed, did not entirely have clean hands.

But my job was not to prosecute tax evasion in Argentina, and my mandate from the judge was not to denounce the investors to the Argentine tax authorities. The authority granted by Judge Kravitz was much more limited, and that's what I told the investors. Their fiscal obligations to their government would have to remain their concern. The report, I told them, was not likely to name them, but would instead list investors in the aggregate, or contain anonymized lists.

One particular investor who sheepishly explained the tax evasion issue to me— which he termed keeping money "en negro," meaning "in black," or undeclared— seemed to have something else on his mind. He didn't say anything specific beyond explaining the tax issue, but it was clear he wanted to say something, but not in front of his fellow investors. So, along with all the brokers I could find and a number of other investors whose information might prove useful, I invited him to come for an interview with Erica and me the next day at the Marval offices in the Buenos Aires "microcenter," or downtown business district. I'll call this investor by the pseudonym Ernesto González.

In the Marval conference room the next day, Mr. González told me the familiar story of how he had met Rolando, been persuaded that he was an investing genius, and given him the better part of his life savings to invest. He had detailed records of how much he had invested and how much he had withdrawn, all of which matched the IATrading.com records. And like the others, he had been convinced that Rolando was making him a steady 1–2 percent return each month, and was having a hard time coming to terms with the reality that he would never see these returns realized. In short, my meeting with Mr. González was utterly uneventful, and told me nothing I didn't know already, which made me think I had simply misread him at the investor meeting. He didn't have anything to say after all.

Then, as he got up to leave the conference room, he made an almost offhand comment: Rolando was "not such a bad guy."

"What do you mean?" I asked. *After all, this guy stole your life savings.*

"Well, he feels really bad, and has been doing his best since all this became public to make things right with some of the investors."

Huh? Was this man in touch with Rolando?

Indeed he was. In response to my rapid-fire questions, as he sat back in his chair, Mr. González explained that he was indeed in touch with Rolando, and that Rolando was in touch with a significant number of other investors as well. Because IATrading.com had been used by some investors as a kind of bank, Rolando kept large amounts of cash in his apartment, which, according to Mr. González, he had been using to repay those investors who had presented the most compelling hardships. And, although he did not know the details, Mr. González said that in addition to returning cash, Rolando had also been making wire transfers. Because my team and I had already seized all the accounts of which we had become aware, containing millions of dollars, I knew that if this was true, this account was new to us. I immediately started to think of ways to find out where it was and get my hands on it.

"You want to meet him?" Mr. González asked me as he wolfed down another pastry.

This was the second moment where initiative came into play. Although the answer to the question was easy—*of course I want to meet him! I've only been trying to contact him for the past several weeks*—the cloak and dagger nature of the proposal Mr. González presented made it harder. Even perilous. He said he had to make a phone call, and returned with very specific instructions. I was to go to a café at an address he wrote on a piece of paper, in a *barrio* that was not familiar to me. Once there, armed with my travel cellphone, I was to sit outside at a table by myself and wait for further instructions. Unless I did it on Rolando's terms, I would not get to speak with him.

I'm convinced that nine out of ten lawyers at large U.S. law firms—who by their nature are risk averse—would have said no. It's not that I ascribe to myself any particular bravery, but I certainly had greater comfort in Argentina and among Argentines than the average American lawyer. And again, it would have been professionally acceptable simply to take the information I had gained from the brokers and the investors, return to the U.S., and put together a distribution plan to present to Judge Kravitz. But more than just my cultural literacy compelled me forward: I remembered well the lessons I had learned all those years ago in the Manhattan DA's office from the veteran investigative ADAs, which I can sum up as "Never stop. Take the next step." In light of that, saying no was not an option.

Before I said yes, Erica looked at me with concern on her face. After all, even though Rolando was technically being *sued* in a civil proceeding rather than *prosecuted* in a criminal case, his conduct was clearly felonious, and he could have been prosecuted in either country had prosecutors taken that initiative rather than the CFTC. I assured Erica that if I went, she would not go with me. Although I didn't think there would be real danger, I couldn't take a chance with a colleague from my firm, and had in any event been instructed to go alone. She made me promise to call her shortly after the appointed meeting time to let her know that everything was all right. With that detail buttoned down, I said yes.

That evening, I took a taxi to the unfamiliar café and, as instructed, sat down outside. After a few minutes, the phone rang. The recognizable voice of Mr. González told me that Rolando would indeed see me, and that I should simply walk inside the establishment, and he would be there. With some hesitation, I went inside, and came face-to-face with the mastermind of the fraud: an out-of-shape, grunge-inspired man in his late 20s, whose baby face made him look even younger. I introduced myself in Spanish.

"Can I see some identification," Rolando asked, sounding surprisingly like a cop at a traffic stop.

"Sure." I handed him my New York driver's license.

He studied the license, and said he was satisfied, but was surprised I didn't have anything that looked more official. To my astonishment, he also asked if I had come to arrest him.

I tried to reassure him. "I'm not a police officer, and I'm not a prosecutor. I'm a lawyer appointed by the court to investigate your case and return money to investors." I also told him that a civil enforcement action is not the same as a criminal matter.

He seemed satisfied. "What do you want to know?"

Now, ordinarily, I would begin an interview at the beginning, and ask him to tell me about the scheme. But here, based on what Mr. González had told me earlier that day, I wanted to get to the heart of the matter: had he in fact been returning money to investors after the court order freezing all his assets? If he had, he would technically have been violating the order, but a contempt proceeding against him was unlikely, and not particularly beneficial to the CFTC's case in any event. Far more consequential was the effect on the investors who might have benefited from this largesse, none of whom bothered to mention it on the questionnaire my team had sent them. If it were true that they had lied, and I could prove it, that would be a bombshell.

I held my breath as I asked about the return of funds, as I knew from long experience that when someone is telling you incriminating things, lots of things can "spook" them. For the same reason, I did not take out a notebook or recording device. It was just him and me, talking over coffee and a snack.

"Yes, of course," he said, seemingly surprised by my asking a question to which he thought I knew the answer. "The truth is I never wanted any of these people to lose money, but when they did, I wanted to make things right to the best of my ability."

This did not shock me. Many investment scammers with whom I've dealt over the years claimed, sometimes truthfully, that in their ideal world, their victims would not lose a cent. The problem is that fraud provisions prohibit materially lying to investors, however much you wished them not to lose money. For the same reason that a stock broker can't take money meant for blue-chip stocks and then bet the entire sum on red at the roulette table, Rolando could not promise safe investments and trade instead in complex derivatives that had a large downside. Nor could he lie to investors about whether the money was in fact kept at a brokerage in Connecticut and was insured by Lloyds of London. He seemed to understand this concept implicitly, not so much making legal excuses as trying to persuade me both that he was not a bad guy, and that his desire to return money was genuine. Because he did not have nearly enough left, he limited the money he returned to hardship cases—as determined by him, naturally.

The biggest revelation was that Rolando had two offshore accounts, one in the Cayman Islands and one in Miami. He had been using those accounts to return money by wire transfer to investors who had invested. For those hardship cases where the original investment had been in cash—usually smaller amounts—he would return money from a dwindling supply of cash that he said he kept at home. Over the next four hours, and again over the next two days at our temporary Buenos Aires headquarters, Rolando walked me through his scheme and the repayments— by wire and in cash—step by step. He did not seek to minimize his culpability, though he placed it in context. I asked him for the account information for his offshore accounts, and he freely gave it. He even brought me the key fob required to access the Cayman account. The only apparent limit to his willingness to cooperate was that he would not tell me where he lived, which I suppose was understandable.

When I told Erica about our conversation the next day, she was astonished at how seemingly forthcoming Rolando had been. And she saw for herself during our two subsequent interviews (Rolando was now more at ease and agreed to confirm additional details at the Marval offices with Erica present) that he was bright, had a good memory, and was obliging with the details about which we peppered him. All told, Rolando had solicited some $43 million in investments based on his misrepresentations, but because he had moved investor money around the various accounts to cover losses, and because the CFTC had stepped in and frozen assets, the investors were out about $20 million. Rolando, as we later calculated, had returned about $2.7 million on his own after the freezing of the accounts, and had less than $500,000 left.

Erica and I left Buenos Aires satisfied that we had come as close to the truth of what happened in the scheme as we could have hoped at the beginning of the assignment. We also left angry that not one investor had mentioned Rolando's apparent largesse, but withheld judgment until the investors had had a chance to come clean. So when we returned to New York, we set out to corroborate Rolando's information. We went through the proper channels, with Rolando's cooperation, to gain access to and freeze the offshore accounts. The account records corroborated what Rolando had said, and gave us a precise road map of the investors who had received wire transfer repayments. We also prepared a second questionnaire to send to all investors. Even though the first questionnaire asked for all funds that had been invested or returned, here we were more pointed, asking whether they had received any repayment of their IATrading funds or knew anyone who had, and whether they had communicated with Rolando, or knew anyone who had.

The return of the second set of questionnaires was demoralizing, but will not surprise seasoned investigators: of more than 30 investors who we established had received post-freeze transfers from Rolando, only a handful truthfully disclosed that fact. With the blessing of the judge, we interviewed all of those who had apparently lied on their questionnaires. After some pointed questioning, all but two confessed to having received money back and lying to the receiver.

The natural question was: now what? How do we deal with Argentine investors who had plainly committed mail or wire fraud by seeking to defraud an American receiver through questionnaires they sent via international wires or international couriers? We could have referred the matter to the U.S. Attorney for criminal prosecution, but because the amount of the discrepancy did not add up to a large sum in any one case (though they did in the aggregate), Judge Kravitz and I came up with a little "rough justice": we would impose a flat $2500 fee on each of the lying investors to defray the costs of my investigation into their fraud, and we would additionally withhold from any distribution 25 percent of the total amount they lied about receiving from Rolando.

This seemed equitable as a punishment but, more importantly, the lying investors did not get an undeserved distribution. As I wrote in my final report to the judge:

> Had the misrepresentations gone undiscovered, the proposed allowed claim amounts for such investors would have been significantly overstated, the effect of which would have been a dilution of distributions to other allowed claimholders and a windfall to the offending claimholders.

In the end, the investors received more than 60 cents on the dollar, which is well above what is typically returned in the aftermath of investment schemes. For certain, it was a satisfying result.

But that result would have been less satisfying and less just had we not taken the initiative to travel to Argentina in the first place, to persist in efforts to locate Rolando, and to go see him and "flip" him. An ordinary investigation ended in an extraordinary outcome.

Advice to Future Investigators

As described above, it is key for investigators seeking the truth in complex matters never to be satisfied with a "check the box" exercise. Instead, and keeping with my training at the hands of the ADAs mentioned above, in the Department of Justice, and in the private sector, I suggest the following (which should, of course, be tailored based on the particular investigation and budgetary realities):

■ If you find one witness, always ask if there are others. Even seemingly uneventful witnesses like Mr. González might have important information.
■ If you get a great statement from a witness, find out if there are ways to confirm externally what the witness is saying. This could be a recording, text message, email, or other corroborative document.
■ If you're wondering how you might establish that someone did or thought something in particular, sometimes the best way is just to ask them (assuming no legal prohibitions, of course).
■ If you have the opportunity to interview a wrongdoer (while of course exercising appropriate caution), take it. Ask them to give you any corroborating evidence they might have, like Rolando's key fob or access to an email account. Many have just been waiting for someone to ask.
■ Sometimes, spending just a bit more money can pay great dividends, as with our trip to Argentina. Find ways to persuade your client of this.
■ If you have subpoena power (such as in civil litigation) don't be afraid to use it appropriately, even if the other side will make a stink. Sometimes, the loudest objections to evidence gathering signal that you have found the most useful evidence.
■ There's often more than one way to skin a cat. Although Rolando did not answer my repeated emails, he agreed to meet because of a relationship with an investor.
■ Last, trust your gut, especially after a few years of experience. Although we would have been fine not to go, we went to Argentina because something seemed too pat, perhaps a bit off. My gut told me to go, and it was a success.

Notes

1. This is an excellent opportunity to give those former ADAs the credit they deserve. From some, I learned directly, and from others, by example: Mike Cherkasky, Leroy Frazer, Owen Heimer, Roslynn Mauskopf, Chris Prather, Pat Dugan, Dan Castleman, and John Moscow. Each contributed in his or her own way to my development as an investigative lawyer, and I am eternally grateful.
2. In addition to the lawyers from the CFTC who worked on and supervised the matter, I credit trial attorneys Michael Berlowitz and Joseph Rosenberg, former prosecutors whom I met as an intern in the New York State Attorney General's Medicaid Fraud Control Unit in 1988, with recommending me for the assignment.

3. To illustrate with a simple example: Investor A invested $80,000 but at some point redeemed $20,000, making his net investment $60,000. Investor B invested $50,000 but at some point redeemed $10,000, leaving him with a net investment of $40,000. That would make the total in the pool $100,000. If ultimately, we succeeded in recovering only $50,000, a *pro rata* distribution would mean that Investor A would receive $30,000 and Investor B $20,000. It's worth noting that, because we would give no credit for fictitious profits, Investor A might well have believed that his account contained $100,000 rather than $60,000, because that is what the IATrading statements provided by Rolando said. In investment schemes that promise outsized returns (this one and Madoff are two examples), this news comes as a great shock to long-term investors.

Chapter 7

Skepticism

Bruce Sackman

Hardly a week goes by without a news story about prescription drug abuse. The statistics are staggering and the stories told by its victims horrific. We read about medical professionals over-prescribing these drugs, about patients shopping for oxycodone and other drugs, or about addicted consumers buying these drugs on the street. Those who divert pharmaceuticals from legitimate sources sometimes make huge profits at the expense of harming or even murdering their customers.

Law enforcement, particularly the Drug Enforcement Administration, has teams of investigators to handle these allegations. However, on occasion a medical center will want to conduct its own internal investigation before calling in the authorities. The allegations may be vague, the chance of unfavorable press high, and outside agencies may uncover even additional wrongdoing.

Performing internal investigations for a large organization requires skills not taught in any investigators' training course that I am aware of. Being a highly trained investigator is of course important, but what is almost equally important is conducting your investigation in a manner that does not cause embarrassment to senior leadership, that does not appear overly aggressive, and that results in improvement to the organization. This is very different from the police investigator who wants to make an arrest and move on to the next case.

On occasion, the target of the investigation will be an individual held in high regard, someone deemed essential for the success of the organization, someone whose character is considered beyond reproach. An anonymous letter or phone call is received via the corporate hotline and the matter must be investigated. No one in the organization is comfortable touching this one.

That's when private investigators can become involved.

In the spring of 2014 the president of a local medical center received an anonymous letter. The allegations contained more questions than answers. The writer alleged that the Director of Pharmacy was signing out oxycodone and amphetamines to a special research pharmacy in the medical center without any accountability by his staff.

That was it. No allegations of personal drug use or diversion, just someone complaining about improper paperwork. After all isn't it the Director of Pharmacy's job to supply these items to the research pharmacy? Let's do an internal investigation before we start calling in the authorities on this anonymous tip, was the unanimous opinion of management.

I had been conducting internal investigations for this medical center for a number of years since my Federal service retirement. As the Special Agent in Charge of the US Department of Veterans Affairs Office of Inspector General for the Northeast, I had seen just about every type of hospital crime there is, from simple theft to homicide. One of the things that I learned over the years is to seek assistance from a professional in whatever field I am investigating. What do I know about being a pharmacist? Not much if anything. In my experience, these experts love a break from their routine duties to play detective, and they are usually pretty good at it. So I grabbed the head of the pharmacy service for the entire hospital network, a highly skilled pharmacist named Joanne, and we took a trip to visit the pharmacist in question.

Most hospital pharmacies look like they were an afterthought when the buildings were planned and designed. They are usually very cramped quarters with some areas more secure than others. Certainly the narcotics are usually pretty secure, but often the high price non-narcotic pharmaceuticals are commingled with the less expensive drugs in a much more open setting.

As we walked through the area you could see pharmacists mixing compounds while nurses and others waited at the window for their prescriptions to be filled. Carts being rolled out the door with drugs for the wards, and a general sense of organized chaos are everyday occurrences.

In the rear of the pharmacy was the director's office. It contained his desk and barely enough room for two chairs. His name was Anthony D, and he had been the Director of Pharmacy for more than five years. After the usual small talk, I told him that an anonymous allegation had surfaced and actually read the allegation to him. He confidently responded something like this:

> Bruce, since 2011 there has been an investigational drug study utilizing oxycodone. That study had recently ended and the records were now in storage; and besides, the research pharmacist involved is currently on vacation anyway. Because of the sensitivity of this study, I took personal responsibility in ordering the drugs, securing it and delivering in the research pharmacy.

I responded by saying that it was a relief to know that the study was in good hands but my boss would require me to review the study and make certain everything was handled in a proper manner. Anthony assured me not to worry, that the DEA frequently conducts drug audits and everything is fine or they would have caught any problems.

I could have easily accepted this explanation as had just about everyone else he provided it to. But an investigator's natural sense of skepticism clawed at me from the moment he confidently supplied it. I don't know if it was his manner of speaking, his lack of eye contact, or just my years of experience that had taught me to verify every claim a potential target of any investigation can make. I learned to be skeptical of every undocumented explanation whether it comes from the Chief Executive Officer or the minimum wage clerk at the front desk.

I insisted that Anthony retrieve the records from storage. Anthony requested that we return next week to review the records and interview the research pharmacist. That was fine with us, but we both left the meeting thinking something was amiss.

The following week Anthony telephoned me and said the records were still unavailable. I told him I would give him a few more days but we were going to return with or without the records to begin the investigation.

Apparently this research study excuse had been good enough for the DEA auditors when they made their routine inspections. Why should I be so skeptical of the Director of Pharmacy who had been a long-time respected member of the management team and passed every DEA inspection?

In my career I have on several occasions documented theft and diversion on the part of individuals considered to be "the most trusted employee". People who are the first to come to work and the last to leave; managers who never want to burden other employees to help them do their job; employees deemed essential, who are considered to "run the place", who never take a vacation, or even a day off, and have exclusive access to certain files and documents as a necessary part of their job, have been led out in handcuffs to the shock of their coworkers. I recall one case of an attorney who was embezzling funds from the estates of his clients. His boss was so convinced that the attorney, whom he had known and worked with for over 20 years, was incapable of such a crime he refused to believe the attorney's guilt until the very day he sat in court and heard this attorney confess his crimes to the judge.

There is an inherent danger in leaving someone in place so long that no one questions his/her job performance. Everyone gets comfortable believing that since nothing to date has gone wrong nothing will go wrong.

Finally I had waited long enough and it was time for me and Joanne to pay Anthony another visit. We entered his office and he seemed okay to see us. I told him we could wait no longer and had to begin interviewing everyone and conducting our investigation. I inquired again about the research study.

Anthony looked at us and said there was no research study and that he had been stealing oxycodone to support his own habit for years. How much oxycodone I asked? Thousands of pills was his response. I glanced over to Joanne and I could see her slumping down on her chair as if she had been hit over the head with a ton of bricks. She looked at me in total shock. But Joanne, being the consummate professional, quickly regained her composure, which began to comfort Anthony.

Anthony said he had considered suicide before our meeting. There was a large window in his office and for a moment I feared he might just jump out. He was a physically large man who worked out frequently lifting heavy weights and there was no way I could successfully hold him back. He asked if he should get a lawyer. This was one of the few times I was glad I was not in law enforcement anymore. I told him that we were not the police and that I represented the medical center so that decision would have to be his alone. Joanne was very concerned about his mental state and assured him that we could arrange for him to see a medical professional. I convinced Anthony to write a statement about this drug diversion and his addiction, which he did.

Joanne and I took Anthony with his statement to see his immediate supervisor, a woman named Deborah. Deborah sat behind her desk and listened to Anthony confess and Joanne reiterate the importance of taking Anthony to employee health because of his statement of contemplating suicide. It was great having Joanne there who was clearly concerned about Anthony's health. Her concern clearly helped convince Anthony to cooperate. Quite frankly at this point I didn't believe anything Anthony said but I wasn't going to mess with someone who says they are suicidal.

We all walked over to employee health, spoke to the physician in charge, filling him in with the details of the day's events and deposited Anthony with him. That would be the last time I would see Anthony until we all sat in the office of the Special Narcotics Prosecutor. Anthony was released from Employee Health after a drug test and evaluation. He tested negative for oxycodone and other prescription or illegal drugs. His stated addiction was just simply another lie to get us to back off pursuing the matter.

Joanne and I immediately returned to the pharmacy and began reviewing the Drug Transaction Review Send Reports to determine the extent of drugs signed-out to the Research Pharmacy by Anthony. The report reflected that from April 2010 (when the system first went on line) to April 2, 2014 Anthony authorized the removal of 155,000 oxycodone pills, 1524 amphetamine pills, and over the last 12 months, 31 testosterone injectable, all supposedly for the research pharmacy. Later on, manual transaction forms for 2009–March 2010 were located reflecting an additional 16,318 oxycodone pills diverted during that time period along with an additional amount of amphetamines.

Anthony even diverted drugs the evening we first interviewed him.

Where did all the drugs go? How did this go on for so long undetected? Where were the supervisors, the auditors, the regulators? Don't we have modern automated systems to track and flag these drug diversions?

The process of ordering narcotics usually begins with the pharmacy technician checking the Par levels to see if there is a sufficient quantity of drugs in stock. If not, the technician will request, in writing, utilizing the correct forms, for the narcotics manager to place the order. One copy of the form is maintained in-house, a copy is sent to the DEA and a copy to the distributor. When the drugs are delivered they are placed into the pharmacy vault. There exists a computerized tracking system known as Pyxis C2 Safe, which stores, tracks and monitors the replenishment of controlled substance inventory within the hospital. In order to remove narcotics, an authorized individual has to enter his user name and password and indicate the specific drug, dosage, schedule, quantity, location user ID and patient name. If the drugs are dispensed from an automated drug machine (Pyxis) a report is automatically electronically generated to indicate how the drug was dispensed.

Here's the problem, there are some departments of the medical center that do not dispense drugs through Pyxis. Reports on how narcotics were dispensed through those sections require a hard copy report. The research pharmacy was a non-Pyxis dispensing department, therefore there were no electronic safeguards in place.

The pharmacy technician told us that, at the request of Anthony, he had ordered oxycodone in amounts from 15 mg to 80 mg beginning sometime in 2010. Anthony told him that the drugs were needed for a specific study being conducted by the research pharmacy. He complained to the narcotics manager he had not received any reports from the research pharmacy regarding its receipt and distribution of oxycodone to patients.

The narcotics manager told us that he began to question Anthony's ordering of these drugs and, in 2012, he told Anthony he would no longer place these orders. Anthony told this narcotics manager that he would do all the ordering himself and handle these products personally.

Finally, the manager of the Research Pharmacy returned to work and told us that from 2010 to the present there were no Research studies requiring the purchasing or dispensing of oxycodone, amphetamines or testosterone. Neither she, nor anyone on her staff, ever requested or received these drugs from the pharmacy for any reason.

A pharmacist assigned to the Research Pharmacy told us that she had no idea that oxycodone pills had been charged out to her service. She had never requested or received any of these pills.

At this point, there was simply no choice but to refer the matter to law enforcement. New York City has a special narcotics prosecutor that handles these types of cases for the entire City. I sent a copy of my report along with the statement Anthony had given us to that office. In short order Joanne and I found ourselves sitting in their conference room with Ryan, their drug diversion prosecutor.

Joanne began explaining the hospital's policies and procedures regarding narcotics and I detailed the investigation. Ryan was pleasantly surprised that we had a signed confession from Anthony. Ryan said we never get signed confessions from anyone in this business, ever.

The next step for me would be to testify to the Grand Jury. Ryan had me come in, and simply asked me to explain to the jurors what had happened. He put me on automatic pilot and for about 30 minutes I related the above story. Shortly thereafter the Grand Jury voted a true bill of indictment, charging Anthony with operating as a major trafficker under the state's Drug Kingpin Statute; he pleaded not guilty. Anthony now faced 15 years to life in prison. Justice A. Kirke Bartley ordered him held on $500,000 bond.

Eventually Anthony agreed to plead guilty and cooperated with the Government. He told us that he had stolen drugs each day by simply putting them into a small paper bag and carrying them out of the hospital. He stated that he had been approached by some individuals where he lived to do this and sold the drugs to them. He spent all the money he had made on a new truck and other personal items. He never used the drugs himself but did give some to his wife to use. Because of his cooperation he was sentenced to five years in jail. This was one of the largest known diversions of oxycodone by a hospital pharmacist and captured headlines around the world. Ryan told me he was contacted by newspapers as far away as New Zealand.

His supervisors all left employment at the medical center before any action was ever taken against them. A new pharmacist was appointed and major changes were implemented to make certain an event like this never occurs again. I learned that the anonymous letter that had started this case was not the first time allegations had surfaced about Anthony's behavior. Back in 2010 an individual came forward alleging that Anthony had been diverting drugs, but the complaints were never fully vetted. Apparently this was not the first anonymous letter either.

Without even the slightest skepticism by the supervisors and most of the staff, Anthony was allowed to continue diverting drugs all while being praised by his unsuspecting supervisors as being an outstanding pharmacist.

Lesson for investigators: skepticism is a healthy and necessary trait in our business. The secret is to politely and respectfully demand the evidence required to corroborate a statement. When and only when you are completely satisfied that the evidence supports your conclusion will your investigative report be a suitable product to present to your clients.

Chapter 8

Discretion

Gareth Howie

Discretion—the noun used to describe the quality of behaving or speaking in such a way as to avoid causing offence or revealing confidential information—is an extremely important quality that an investigator needs in order to carry out his or her work.

Have I personally and professionally always been discreet or held my actions to the utmost discretion? Truthfully? No. And as my wife will undoubtedly attest, when my children are in bed and I've pulled a cold can of Pabst Blue Ribbon from the fridge, no one probably loves a good gossip at the end of a long day as much as I do. Personally, I love to hear what friends within our circle are up to, who is annoying who and who has fallen out with who. And, if the true definition of discretion does indeed involve possessing the quality of speaking in such a way as to avoid causing offence, anyone who's ever asked what I think of their outfit or haircut may become passionate in refuting any notion that I possess it.

Professionally, however, I had to learn the hard way about the perils of indiscretion, and to develop a better understanding and awareness of the importance of being discreet. Luckily I learned very early on the hard way, and have been able to apply that lesson accordingly.

Here is an example. When I was a young probationary police officer (in the policing era, pre-smart phones) I had been involved in the arrest of a prominent criminal, well-known within the community I policed. I was buzzing with adrenaline because it was a strong, high profile arrest for a probationer to be involved in. That night after finishing my shift, I went across town to meet friends and fellow police officers in a bar where I was congratulated for the arrest. I was riding the 'high' even a few beers down and started to tell a few of my colleagues that the arrest was "just the beginning." I'd been told by CID a raid was being planned on the home of the arrestee's mistress where they expected to find "even more drugs."

Naturally, my conversation was not private. With the sort of 'small-world or what?' craziness usually reserved for second act twists in bad TV police procedurals,

I was overheard quite clearly throughout by someone in the bar who knew someone who knew someone ... you get the picture. By the time I had finished my next few pints of beer and continued to drunkenly ramble, word had circulated back within the arrested individual's "community." Wouldn't you know it; his mistress' house was 'clean as a whistle' by the next morning—a fact that flew in the face of the strong intelligence the police had received the night before.

I learned a valuable lesson that day. Questions were asked, aspersions were cast, and me and my big mouth took the hit for the horrifying levels of indiscretion. I garnered a (thankfully short-lived) bad reputation amongst my police colleagues. It hit me hard to know that I had impacted something so important so enormously with such a stupid, careless action. But significantly it opened my eyes to why discretion is imperative. I permanently changed my actions going forward.

A seasoned police officer I worked with not long after that drunken 'big mouth' incident, gave me a great piece of advice when it comes to discretion in investigation. Regarding information, he said the sharing process is "'need to know' [in basis] and you are the one to decide who needs to know!" This is sage advice for any investigator.

To work in my field without discretion would involve you showing your subjects your complete investigative process. These actions would serve to possibly enlighten future 'subjects of enquiry' to your intentions along your investigatory pathway. As I learned to my detriment with the aforementioned example—giving a target or subject the chance to destroy or conveniently 'lose' key evidence you're wanting to acquire, or signal to others that you're on the case, is ruinous to any investigation.

Discretion is important in many professions and fields. I am unfamiliar with any poker player who's ever won big from showing what they're holding from the outset. Just like I am unfamiliar with any investigator who puts their entire set of 'tells' or investigative clues, out on display without a care. Similarly, I don't know many investigators who've managed to successfully resolve their cases and retain and attract a strong client base without being immensely discreet.

The latter is an important component, so we'll spend a brief moment discussing it.

Especially in the field of private investigation, the vast majority, if not the entirety, of the investigator's client-base, will expect the utmost discretion and confidentiality at all times. Particularly, private clients with personal problems. In the cases of a cheating partner investigation, for example, the client may not want it ever becoming apparent that they hired a private investigator. The investigator may not find any evidence of infidelity. Discretion is imperative in this case, to keep the client's relationship intact. With a commercial client, the organization may not want the full details of the investigator's intentions to be known. If the suspect is aware they are being investigated, the organization runs the risk of displacing the misconduct said investigator was hired to capture evidence of in the first place.

I developed my ability to be discreet by, to put it bluntly, learning to shut my mouth and open my ears more. As I developed my skills as an investigator out of the police and into the civilian sector, it became very apparent that the more you are trusted as an investigator, the greater the workflow that comes your way. The trust is built off of your ability to garner what is required as discreetly (and often as quickly) as possible.

By the time I came to set up my own company specializing in professional investigation in multiple forms, I was well versed in what private individuals and commercial companies, along with solicitors and insurers, wanted most from an investigator, working lawfully. And that was an investigator who was discreet. This is absolutely the case in the field of fraudulent injury/claim investigation work for insurance firms, where you will be expected to work with the utmost discretion from the outset. Discretion is required in order to achieve multiple visits/acts of surveillance and gather the maximum range of footage pertaining to said injury/claim over many days.

I highly value the importance of discretion. Therefore my organization was built with a strict ethos that, whatever I find as an investigator, the only person who needs to see it is the person who has hired me to find it. Only with their permission does it filter out to anybody else. We underpin this within my company by never discussing active cases with anyone other than the client themselves. Whether this be at a business networking event, or a professional seminar, etc. It doesn't matter if the names, places are changed. We don't discuss it. Nor when we're doing our marketing do we utilize any case or operation for 'case studies' and the like that have occurred within a preceding six-month window.

You can develop the skill-set of discretion as an investigator by being mindful of your professional actions and interactions. In all interactions, you should be sure that you are *receiving* more information and intelligence than you're *giving out* in every interaction.

The following questions can serve as a guide. In all situations, ask yourself the following:

- Does the person I'm speaking to need to be made aware of more than they know already?
- Does it need to be me that does this? If not, should someone else on my team handle this?
- What is the benefit of me doing this?
- What does the investigation gain, from me doing this?
- What can it lose, doing this?
- Can I get what I need from this person by alternative means/questions without divulging more information than I wish to?

Investigators can always maintain their own discretion, but their clients are another story. Discretion is most definitely a two-way route between the investigator and their client. Here is an example of how a client's lack of discretion can compromise an investigation.

Recently, a client hired us because she was convinced her husband of many years was cheating on her with one of his customers. She'd screenshot all the incriminating messages of him and his 'lady friend' off of his mobile phone after finding out his pin code. As a result she came to learn which hotel on the Scottish Borders the two would be going to that weekend.

She hired myself and my team because she wanted the so-called "money shot"— that photograph or video footage of the two together in a romantic embrace or acting as a couple. I and one other operative went up to the location. One of us worked the exterior, ready to 'trigger' arrivals, and one worked the interior, ready to take the departure. We waited, waited and waited some more. The target did not arrive. The mistress did not arrive.

We updated the client of "no action to report." She immediately called us up and said "Yeah, I didn't think he'd show up after all." I asked why, and she replied

> We had a barnstormer of an argument last night. I told him I was onto him. I told him I knew the name of his mistress. That I knew where he was going to meet her that weekend and how I had PIs ready to catch him at it too! He'd have been mad to show up knowing I had people waiting!

We were incredulous. The client said she couldn't help blurting everything out in anger and she regretted it. She didn't cancel us on the off-chance he called her bluff and went ahead with his planned tryst anyway. Here, the client's inability to maintain discretion ultimately cost her the important confirmatory evidence she sought in the first place.

Trust is the foundation of discretion. To put it simply, discretion births trust, and in our line of work trust goes a long, long way—especially when it comes to repeat business and developing professional relationships.

I have another example demonstrating the value of discretion in the investigative process. Here, you'll see just how much we were able to achieve without becoming exposed or our actions becoming public to the investigatory subjects themselves, due to our discretion.

In early 2018, we completed a case for a major national organization with multiple offices. Their requirement from the outset was that discretion was absolutely paramount. We delivered results with the utmost discretion for this client. It is a terrific example for you, in that we got a lot of positive feedback from our work on this matter, which earned us a tremendous run of word-of-mouth referrals from this organization to their business partners and beyond. In the following case study, the actual names and identities have been changed.

We were hired by a company called 'Infinity.' Infinity was a designer and manufacturer of a specific type of high-end computer servers and had offices in London, Manchester, Edinburgh and Newcastle.

Infinity was facing the possibility of making a series of redundancies across their sites. They were in discussions with one of the executive officers at the Newcastle office, a man named 'William,' as to the best method going forward in order to execute this. At the same time, Infinity itself was growing concerned about William's own expenses. They were worried about the "confusion" that was happening, between the large sums of money in restaurants/bars that he was charging as "meeting expenses" and the absence of tangible "meetings" they could tie the costs to.

Infinity executives had spoken informally with William about their concerns, and he always had an explanation ready. He made several grand claims about business meals, and nights out in the city with other executives from various companies, etc. All with the intent of getting a business deal going for Infinity. All interactions failed to generate any successful partnership going forward.

Infinity's head of accounts and its head of HR were rightly suspicious. They got the company's HQ to sanction an independent investigation into the 'movements' on William's company credit card. The caveat was that the investigation needed to be proportionate, speedy and, most importantly, incredibly discreet. The company feared that should an independent investigation yield nothing of detriment, and William was to find out about it, he may leave, and try to take action against the company for constructive dismissal.

Infinity's head of HR asked us to consult on this case and lead the independent investigation into William's spending. We took a drop sample of three incidents of concern to the company. One in particular was an overnight stay in a hotel in the city center charged by William to Infinity. This expense didn't make sense because he lived just over ten miles from that location with his wife and children.

William, a gentleman in his mid to late 50s, was asked about paying for a hotel room on the company credit card when he lived locally. He explained that he had a series of alcohol-driven, late-night networking events at that location, and he thought it easier to stay over. He explained that he did not want to go home and disturb his family in the late evening. He reasoned that he would also be closer to work, which would allow him to arrive on time only hours later. He also said that, on a number of occasions, he had paid for managing directors to come up to the region and stay overnight to see the city as guests of Infinity.

Once our investigation commenced, William's story started to fall apart. Very quickly we were able to ascertain that local companies William had said he had been meeting with (for expensive meals on the Quayside to discuss business proposals) had never actually heard of him. They had also, in some cases, never heard of Infinity. Representatives were very happy to sign statements attesting to this.

While our investigation was discreetly moving forward in this capacity, redundancies were being actioned at Infinity. William was said to be managing the process at the Newcastle site in partnership with an external organization. The intended practice was that Infinity's HR team would correlate all employee statistics based around length of service, continued professional development, disciplinaries, etc., and pass that information on to William. William would liaise with the external organization who would use their own matrix system to independently draw up who the 'suitable' candidates for redundancy were. William would then use their results as the basis for his short-list.

As this was occurring, we now had evidence that strongly indicated William's credit card usage was not legitimate. The date and time for receipts involving the overnight hotel stay included a meal in the hotel's restaurant. We used the recorded date and time as a basis to approach the hotel under the guise of looking into a "theft" that had occurred from my wife's jacket while she had been dining that night. Looking through the CCTV footage from the restaurant we were able to spot William and the person he was dining with, and procure a screengrab of the two of them together.

On the same day that we met with our clients at Infinity, William announced five members of staff who would be facing redundancy out of the Newcastle office. Allegedly, on being presented with the news, one of the selected five turned to the head of HR and said, "Maybe if I was going to The Copthorne Hotel for private staff appraisals with one of the bosses, I'd not be losing my job either!"

This confused and confounded the head of HR—until hours later when we sat down with her and the head of accounts again to talk through our initial findings. At this stage in our investigation, the woman dining with William in the screengrab was immediately identified as a junior member of staff within the organization named 'Elizabeth,' a lady in her late 20s to early 30s. The head of accounts at Infinity suggested that with both William and Elizabeth being married, with William lying about who he was dining with, this had the appearance of an extramarital affair. More pertinently, they were using Infinity's company expense account to pay for it.

Over the course of the next few days, and with the utmost discretion, I worked with Infinity to review the concerned expenditures along with William and Elizabeth's calendared records. We were able to very quickly spot a pattern—the same day on the third week of every month seemed to be highlighted time and again as a peak period of questionable expenditure by William on the company credit card.

The head of accounts wanted to move ahead with suspension and disciplinary action immediately. I called for Infinity to hold back on that action in the first instance. My argument was that we had a lot of strong evidence regarding William's actions but there was the possibility of making it even stronger. I revealed that both William and Elizabeth had made diary entries for a week later, for what might be another illicit liaison, which would put them together at the company's expense, on company time, during hours when they should be working.

A meeting was arranged with the upper management team at Infinity HQ. It was agreed that surveillance would be authorized on both William and Elizabeth for a week's time. The sole purpose of the surveillance was to proportionately monitor what unauthorized spending occurred between the two of them on the company credit card.

There was an additional twist in this case. While we were working on follow-up enquiries and intelligence-gathering ahead of the surveillance, I woke suddenly in the middle of the night with a revelation. It seemed very cliché—I was the investigator who had an 'awakening' with that one big clue or revelatory line of enquiry they'd let slip by—just like I had seen on television. This situation reminded me of that final moment in *The Usual Suspects* when Chazz Palminteri looks at the notice board. But it happened to me in real life. I thought to myself "When that staff member talked about 'private staff appraisals with one of the bosses', could she have been onto something more than she realized?"

I wanted to act on this immediately. I got up at three in the morning, fired up my laptop and sent an email out to the Head of HR at Infinity (because nothing shows manic dedication to your client quite like corresponding with them in the early hours of the morning). I suggested that we ask the external organization who consolidated the redundancy data to send their original results, but this time, direct to her, and then run the matrix again.

Two days later, my random middle-of-the-night moment of inquisitiveness paid off. It was confirmed that the information presented to William about applicable candidates for redundancy had been altered by him before being passed to the Human Resources team. It was altered by one name.

As expected, the original fifth name for suggested redundancy that was now missing from the final list, only to be replaced by someone else's, was Elizabeth's. William had falsified the document and indicated that a different staff member was more applicable for redundancy, based off the indexed employee statistics, rather than the member of staff that he was having an affair with.

Another hastily arranged meeting was convened. We were asked to present everything we had to the head of HR, the director of Infinity, and his national team. We did, and the feeling was universal that William was to be suspended immediately. "What if he claims that it was a typo or a mistakenly sent document or … something like that?" I asked the room. The cacophony of voices that came back all seemed to eventually convolve into a chorus of agreement that there'd been no way William "could talk his way out of this" and the "expenses debacle is one thing" but "this is different."

I needed to convince them to let me collect more evidence. I stood up, readjusted my PowerPoint presentation back to the most pertinent point, and gave my counter-argument.

> It feels to me that we've uncovered what his intent is—and that's to protect a particular member of staff, favoring her unjustly over others in the matter of impending redundancy. We are all sat here with the belief that we know what his motive is too—and that's to protect the particular member of staff because he is having an affair with her and using company resources to do so. But, if we're really honest, the only evidence we have in terms of the motive is this.…

I refocused everyone's attention back on the screengrab of CCTV footage from the hotel restaurant.

... and I think that this on its own is not a whole lot. It's two work colleagues having a meal at the end of the day. And rather naughtily getting their employers to pay the bill. We all know what they're up to. But proof of it is different. And I think the proof is just a few days away if I'm right in what I have predicted about their movements.

They seemed receptive to my argument. The room was silent for what felt like minutes, but it was realistically only a matter of seconds, before Infinity's director spoke. He explained that he didn't like the idea of placing members of his company under surveillance, yet also he felt a strong argument had been put forward for its need. He deferred to the company's legal counsel, also in the room at this time, and the meeting was momentarily adjourned so they could talk. Upon their return, the director said

I acknowledge what you're saying about the need to prove motive, so to speak. But for me, there is no justification for William to have spent the thousands he has so far for legitimate professional purposes. I feel we have a strong case as it stands but I think it could be absolutely irrefutable with evidence of them meeting up together on company time and spending company money to indulge in inappropriate conduct with one another.

This meeting's conclusion highlighted the importance of discretion. Infinity was clear that their end intention was to summarily dismiss both members of their staff. However, they also wanted to ensure the staff member wrongly targeted for redundancy was never made aware of the fraud putting them in that circumstance. Furthermore, they were explicit in stating that there could be no risk of William or Elizabeth becoming aware at any time that they were under surveillance. We had to give our client the utmost assurances that we would be able to conduct the entirety of our surveillance operation with no risk of exposure, and a guarantee of a complete abort at the first sign of the merest possibility of it.

We worked to gather our evidence. First, the statements. We prudently secured a signed statement of fact from an alleged business associate of Infinity. This was a person William claimed to have: met with, had meals with, discussed partnership opportunities with, and most importantly, stayed overnight in hotels as a guest of Infinity. His statement contained a clear declaration that he had never met with William on any of the suggested dates or times, and had never entertained business opportunities with Infinity in the manner William had previously stated.

Next, a report from the company that provided the statistics for the redundant candidate selection. We asked them to compile and submit a detailed report containing their original findings and the methodology they employed, who they sent it to at Infinity, the time and date of their submission, and an attestation that the results William had presented were not the original report they submitted.

Finally, surveillance footage. We worked discreetly with Infinity's HR team and their IT specialist to correlate the surveillance footage we recorded and the evidence we procured against the dates and times of emails William and Elizabeth had sent, meetings they calendared that suggested they were in one place, (when we knew them to be in another), etc.

And with all of that put together, and the suggested period of the next available rendezvous between them approaching, a fellow surveillance operative and I set a plan in motion. We would work on gathering what we felt was the final piece of evidence to wrap this whole thing up narratively and evidentially, the way we would have liked.

The day was here, and we were ready. It was that "same day on the third week of every month" when Elizabeth and William were scheduled to meet. Elizabeth had confirmed on her work calendar that she was going from lunch, to a "mentor meeting" with William, and then on to pick up some printing from a professional outlet in town. She had herself marked as returning to the office at 1600 hrs for a 1700 hrs finish. William, on the other hand, had himself at work until 1330 hrs, at a "staff mentor meeting" and then in Durham for the rest of the afternoon to pitch to new prospective clients.

The surveillance began with William. At 1220 hrs, William left work and I "picked him up" (started following him) outside in the forecourt where I tailed him covertly through the city, to the same hotel that he had previously frequented with the company credit card. I recorded him taking a table in the hotel restaurant at the exact moment my colleague informed me that he "had movement on" (was watching) Elizabeth leaving work, 20 minutes or so later.

My colleague then followed Elizabeth. He secured footage of her walking from work to the same hotel, and he handed her off to me as she entered the hotel. I then watched and took covert photographs of the two of them meeting and dining together for lunch.

As lunch was coming to an end, William went over to reception. My colleague shoulder-surfed him successfully enough to hear him book a room at the hotel, for one night, and hear which room he had been given (625). This information was passed to me via text message and I moved off from my position in the restaurant and took my place on the sixth floor corridor just outside the elevators.

The surveillance then moved toward the hotel room. With the meal finished, William and Elizabeth headed out of the restaurant and towards the elevator, which they took to the sixth floor. My colleague had notified me of their movements, so by the time they came out of the elevator, I had positioned myself further along the corridor. I was bent down over my bag with my back to them, pretending to take something from it. On the ground next to me, pointing down the corridor towards them, and specifically at Room 625, was my covert takeaway coffee cup camera, recording time- and date-stamped coverage in full high definition.

Next, we got the proverbial "money shot." We captured William and Elizabeth coming out of the elevator together holding hands, stopping at Room 625. William unlocked the door, while Elizabeth groped him from behind. They went into the room together and closed the door. Neither parties exited the hotel room again within their working hours. Elizabeth in fact called the office to inform them she would not be returning, as her "husband was stuck at work and unable to pick up the children as planned."

Our surveillance continued outside their hotel rendezvous. They eventually exited the room at 1930 hrs when they both went downstairs, had a meal in the restaurant, and then returned back to their room. Our client told us to stop surveillance and we returned immediately to Infinity's offices. We worked into the night, editing our video footage, finalizing our report and submitting our supporting photographs.

The next day, Infinity was ready to confront Elizabeth and William. My colleague and I were put on stand-by with Infinity in case we were required to supplement our evidence with personal testimony ("the absolute worst case scenario" according to the head of Infinity). William and Elizabeth were called in to a meeting with Infinity's HR and legal team, presented with all of our evidence, and summarily suspended pending a disciplinary hearing for gross misconduct.

They each had very different reactions to the evidence. Elizabeth said that she was in love with William. She also said they were planning on leaving their partners to be together. She didn't want their new relationship to start "under a cloud" so she resigned immediately. She also knew she was likely to be terminated, following Infinity's hearing.

William, however, claimed to be the 'victim' of a 'honey trap' situation. He said Infinity used Elizabeth to seduce him, as an excuse to fire him, so they would not have to pay his company bonus. He said he planned to leave the company and sue them. He stormed out of the meeting room, where he was apparently met by police officers, waiting to speak to him about his misuse of the company's credit card. Our evidence report was used by the police when interviewing William.

The following day, William spoke with Infinity's designated liaison. Ultimately, a settlement was reached. Infinity would drop the charges against him, in return for his resignation and repayment of the money spent. Presumably, William's desire was to hide this entire saga as best possible from his wife and family. Court appearances, media interest and the like were not amenable to his plan.

Our client, Infinity, was delighted with the result achieved by us. Our adherence to our code of discretion was the greatest measure of our success in this investigation. Given the potential strength of office gossip, it was amazing that no one ever found out the lengths we went to in order to expose William's fraudulent conduct and illicit behavior with Elizabeth. No one outside the trusted circle of the Infinity management team were ever actually aware that an outside professional investigation service was working to gather evidence. The targets were never informed about our investigation, which allowed us to get video surveillance footage. The staff member who was put forward for unjust redundancy by William, never knew what went on behind the scenes, and was not adversely affected. Consequently, this case serves as a great example to any investigator learning to properly employ discretion over the course of a surveillance operation.

Chapter 9

Adaptability

Cynthia Navarro

My professional career trajectory as an investigator demonstrates my personal adaptability. I have worked in several investigative capacities over the years, and performed my job using many different modalities. I started out as an undercover investigator, then worked as a background check investigator, and today I manage high technology cases. My career has spanned several distinct eras, (1970s–present) and thus my techniques evolved along with it. I think you will enjoy reading my story which demonstrates the importance of being adaptable as an investigator.

Adaptability. This one word describes an important skill which a successful investigator must have. The best definition I've found for adaptability is: an ability to change or be changed in order to fit or work better in some situation or for some purpose.[1]

My story in adaptability as an investigator started with my initial intent to go to law school. As you will see, I completely adapted my intended career path to an entirely new career objective. One day, while waiting to get a law school application, I was browsing a bulletin board, and there it was—an advertisement looking for a part-time investigator. This was a perfect opportunity for me, as I was still in school, completing my senior year. At this time, I had already been working part-time as an undercover investigator for a California state agency. However, the work was sporadic, and I really needed to make additional money, so another part-time job in this industry sounded ideal. I grabbed both the advertisement and my application for law school. Little did I know at that moment; my dream of law school would soon fade.

I got that part-time investigator job and ultimately completed my Bachelor of Science degree in Criminal Justice. Despite starting that job as a part-time employee, I worked my way up in the company to become a manager. For the next nine years I had a very exciting career. I worked for the same Vice President, in three different companies. I also reached a very important milestone in the process. In this organization, which had over 80 offices, I became the very first female investigative manager.

In 1989, I obtained my private investigator's license. Although it sounds like a glamorous career path, it wasn't all fun and games. I worked extremely hard, constantly adapting my skill-set to my environment. Like many new investigators, I hit the ground running. There was no training or adjustment period. I was essentially told to "run and figure it out as you go" and the ability to adapt to my given situation served me very well.

Starting with my first investigative job, I was constantly adapting to the evolving technology. You will see from this story how investigations have evolved with the advent of technology. While attending college, I worked part-time as an undercover investigator with a state agency. The process went something like this. They would call me on my telephone at home and provide me with the background information I needed to get started, which I wrote down using pencil and paper. We would make plans to meet in an area close to the location where I needed to go perform undercover work. At that time, it was very important to get the meeting location correct, because it was difficult to contact the person once you left the house—your only option was a public pay phone (you needed to have plenty of loose change handy!), and if the person had already left their house, you would be unlikely to reach them. This would be terrible, because you didn't want to miss meeting with your backup. (As an undercover, it is very important to have someone close by your assignment to serve as a backup.)

Next, I would perform my assignment, and return to a previously agreed upon meeting location to provide a verbal update to my supervisor. Then, I would create a hand-written report in the car. Later, when performing investigative work for corporations, I "advanced" to the latest technology: an electric typewriter and lots of White-Out. (This was a tiny bottle of white liquid that you would brush over your typing mistake so it blended into the paper, and you could retype over it. This was as much work as it sounds like! Later, they made something called white tape, which made corrections a lot easier.) In the mid-1980s computers started to appear in offices. However, they were in short supply. During this time, I now had an assistant, with a computer (this was the only computer in the entire office!) who helped me type my reports. The investigative process kept adapting and evolving.

With the advent of the computer, I decided to adapt my investigative career accordingly. At this time, my boss, a forward-thinking, adaptable man, speculated we would all have computers on our desks. Most people would not have thought this at the time. While loving my career path, moving forward with the technological changes made life much easier. I realized that I needed to really understand technology, and fully educate myself in it, or I would be left behind. Today, I realize my ability to adapt to the latest technology was an astute career move. Now, I am a computer expert and I'm enjoying an exciting niche career in high technology investigations, serving clients in myriad industries.

Being from a military family, I learned the art of adaptability at a young age. You can't survive countless moves to new housing, friends, schools and different towns without the keen sense of adaptability. I moved as many as seven times in a

12-year period. The field of investigations is quite similar. In one week, you might work a variety of cases, going from a business background case, to a copyright case, to an employee theft case. Accordingly, your skill level bounces back and forth from one case to another. You will come to find that everyone wants their case, matter or task completed right away. Today. How you manage your time and skill-set in the service of multiple, competing, tight deadlines can be both a bewilderment and amazement. You will never have the opportunity to give up; throwing up your hands and saying "forget it" if you want to stay prosperous in this business. To that end, an important tool for every investigator is the ability to adapt your skills and time management to serve the tasks at hand.

The business of investigations is best suited for someone with an adaptable personality. I believe that it's easy to get overwhelmed if you tend to be rigid, inflexible and uncompromising. An example would be going into a case and finding what was once an easy task, has suddenly changed and became cumbersome. Or, realizing that some form of technology could make your life easier, and best serve your case, but it is difficult to understand. That sudden change can restrict some people from moving forward and might even push them ten steps back. If you are inflexible, how can you move forward and accomplish your task. Do you stop and say "I can't do this" and end the task? There are people that ask themselves this very question in every industry, every single day. But in investigations, the answer is no, you move forward. Yes, you may pause for a few beats while you stop to look around the hurdle for more options, and ask yourself or someone else about possible alternatives. But investigators don't give up. Don't ever just give up. I never gave up. My personal ability to remain adaptable facilitated my growth in the area of technology.

As an investigator, it is also important to be constantly learning new things and remaining open to networking opportunities. I belong to an organization called the High Technology Crime Investigation Association (HTCIA). I joined in 1992, and while I wasn't sure what they were all about at the time, it ended up being one of the best moves I've made in my career. This organization brings law enforcement, prosecutors and corporate investigators together. Education and networking are the prime goals.

The power of investigative networking is evident in the following story involving a friend of mine. One day I was having lunch with some fellow HTCIA members. We were chatting and one guy said he was thinking about switching jobs and going to work with a new company. He told us the company was looking for someone to start a security team and they were looking for candidates. He wasn't sure about taking the job, because he had been with his current position for a few years already, and it was a stable company. We had all heard of this new company, and discussed the pros and cons of the new position. The consensus was that he should take a risk, and just go for it. We thought it sounded like a great opportunity; a totally different career path for him, where he could grow and adapt to a new and different company culture. He took the job a week or so later and ended up doing very well. We now know what a fantastic decision that really was. That company is Google.

Working in Silicon Valley, especially in the beginning, was best suited for people that were adaptable. It was a new era of companies, coworkers and CEOs. With so many new technology companies beginning, such as Google, Facebook, LinkedIn, Twitter, it was a whirlwind of startups. The culture was filled with risk-takers ready to take on the world, and immerse themselves in change. Some companies' mottos were to jump over hurdles, make mistakes, and not look back. This was a new pioneering frontier. It became a challenge, yet was exciting, for investigators. We really needed to hop on the wagon and understand exactly what these technology companies were all about. Security, law enforcement and investigators really needed to work together. Security was implementing control, providing badges, using cameras, developing policies and company relationships. Investigators needed to understand their capabilities to conduct investigations. Law enforcement needed to understand the technology in order to fully understand what they were investigating. They also needed to understand that they were working with a newer and much younger generation. This generation didn't have time to consider risks that were emerging, as they were working exhausting hours to produce and innovate. Security was not always top of their minds when considering intellectual property, trade secrets, brand protection and more.

Anyone that could not adapt to this environment was left behind. This was a world where anyone who was rigid, inflexible and uncompromising would not do well. It was obvious. It was a particular challenge for investigators coming from a law enforcement or military background. Their careers were based on policies, strict guidelines and rigid leadership. Their challenge was learning to talk to a new generation of subjects as well as employees. An authoritative approach was not always the best approach, and for those who chose it routinely, it harmed the investigative outcomes. All investigators are wise to remember that subjects are usually best approached in an open and friendly manner. People generally need to feel comfortable in order to share information. To this end, in the corporate world, traditional investigative terms are often not used. For instance, investigations can be called "research" and interrogations are instead referred to as "interviews."

I remember one time I was called in to conduct an interview instead of another investigator. That investigator was a skilled, former police officer, who had more experience than me. Naturally, I was puzzled, and wondered why they asked for me instead of him. I asked my supervisor. At the time, I was surprised by the answer. My supervisor said the other guy was using a very authoritative approach and Human Resources were concerned about how the interview would be conducted. My supervisor knew another technique was needed, because we were hoping to get information from the suspect, without him realizing he was the suspect. This was to appear as a friendly, informational, low-key conversation.

I'll provide you with some of the highlights of what ended up being a very long interview. This story illustrates the value of using a very simple but effective investigative technique where you attempt to solicit "help" from the subject during the interview process. Perhaps it will help you, if you are a new investigator.

I started our discussion very slow and easy, by reviewing his employment history with the company. I let him know I did not have experience in his field, and that I might ask questions that seemed unnecessary, but I would depend on him to correct me. Ultimately, it was important this employee didn't think he was under suspicion. He was arrogant and cocky, which made matters difficult, but my ultimate goal was to have him help me. That was my hook—and it worked. I needed his help to understand processes and procedures. We chatted, and in this process I was being educated by someone who acted quite superior to me. He liked showing how much he knew. It was working perfectly. I went as far as asking how he would investigate this type of situation because I was not sure what direction to take. He responded just as I had hoped; verifying what he would do, and why. However, I had done my homework and so I knew what he was leaving out. Of course, he didn't want to implicate himself so I kept listening and nodding. I would repeat the things he said, to ensure I was understanding him correctly. He was confident and at ease during the entire conversation.

Then I got a great result, using another common investigative technique to help elicit a possible confession. This technique entails taking a large box of "evidence" related to the case (which can be any materials at all—it doesn't have to be actual evidence) that you place near the subject and discuss during questioning. The idea is to make the defendant think there is a mountain of evidence related to his/her case so they confess to their crime quickly, rather than waste investigators' time.

To this end, I started pulling "evidence" out of a box that was next to me; items such as video cartridges, files of computer logs, and emails. Some items had evidentiary value; others did not. I told him the videos showed him entering a secured lab, as someone was leaving. Meanwhile, it is important for me to note that we did not know this for sure, but we believed it was the only way he could have entered a lab without proper access (which he did not have). Yet the video tapes in question were actually blank. The computer logs provided dates and times of logins for a specific computer where information had been downloaded to a thumb drive. The emails were from his company computer, which contained some incriminating statements. I had a few other files which were somewhat relevant to the case, but it all helped to look like a lot of information. Plus, I spoke confidently about the information I had. We really only had a small amount of data from his emails that had been captured by our data loss prevention software, which is used to track outgoing emails with company confidential information. We had yet to investigate how the information could be accessed, where it was stored and who had access before we even started the interview. The suspect helped by showing his knowledge of a system and a process. It was just enough to let us know he was capable of accessing information he should not have had. We filled in the blanks and in the end, he gave us a confession.

There were a few key elements that made this interview a success. First, the investigative supervisor understood the best approach for the interview and staffed it accordingly. Second, the interviewing investigator listened, watched and adapted to the suspect's demeanor throughout the interview. Finally, the interviewer (although it didn't appear this way to the subject) quietly had command of the interview from the beginning.

Investigative department structure is another factor that can influence investigative outcomes. The investigative function in a given organization can be organized in many different ways. As an investigator, I have personally been organized under departments such as Facilities, Human Resources, Legal, Marketing and Sales. How you are organized can be an important factor in your work, because it can affect your investigative goals. You should always ask yourself a few key questions, such as: how does your work benefit or interest them? Do you get rebuttal when you bring a case forward? Do they understand the importance of the issue at hand and how it affects the company? How interested in a given case is the individual who oversees the department? Ideally, regardless of the department in which you are organized, you will have great support, serving as cheerleaders in the background, making noise, and with unwavering backing for your work. Once you have upper management support, this will assist others in understanding that what you do is important for the company which will assist you in your investigations.

Another group you will want to have supporting you is the investigative administrative support staff (admin). They are the folks who manage the managers, and they are true assets for the investigator. You will need their cooperation and assistance to get meetings set, assist in pushing your agenda with supportive conversations, advise you of the best person in a group to approach, and the best way to approach them, etc. Keep in mind that they don't have to work with you directly in the same company, to offer assistance.

I have a great example of admin adding value to my investigation and helping me to adapt to new situations. My problem was adapting to working with law enforcement staff. In rectifying this problem, I realized the value of social skills, and their importance to my investigations. At one time, I was performing contract work for several software and hardware companies regarding counterfeiting, brand protection and trademarks. During this time, software came in boxes, in the form of CDs and manuals. The hardware side was new, and moving fast. It was not unusual for me to assist Federal, State, and Local law enforcement in search warrants to identify counterfeit product versus genuine product. I was a good source, as my expertise in this field assisted them in identifying several software and hardware products.

To this end, I was asked to participate in the preparation of several search warrants. I learned many valuable investigative lessons while performing this type of work. For instance, I learned it's important to have respect for your skill-set when joining in on a search warrant. You are working fast, determining what can sometimes be an overwhelming amount of product to be identified. When identifying counterfeit items, you have to look for minor details, such as misspelled word(s), blurred print, wrong font, determining whether it was a pressed disc (from a manufacturer) or a burned disc (from a computer) among other identification techniques. Generally, it's the inconsistences with packaging, colors, trademarks, unauthorized dealer/ sellers and other visual knowledge that are not public information, which help to identify the fakes.

I also learned the value of having strong relationships with your counterparts on these operations. There are a few ways to achieve this. One is to follow directions carefully and to stay out of the way of the officers/agents. Overall, I have great respect for the officers/agents I work with. I have taken the time to understand their expectations and adapt gracefully to their various nuances.

However, there was one agent that would literally ignore me. I encountered this individual often, so I made a special effort to get along. I tried using my best communication skills. Yet it didn't seem to work, no matter what I tried. Then one day I was talking to an admin on this agent's team. I explained to her that I had no idea what I had done for him not to talk to me. In response, she simply looked at me and laughed, telling me that it was not me, personally, but that he was a bit shy. She said to get him to open up to me, all I needed to do was ask about his kids. That was it. So, the next time I ran into the agent, I did exactly what she said, and I asked him about his kids. To my surprise, this worked. We ended up having a brief conversation, talking about children, and soon we were like old friends. All from one special question. I was thankful for the advice from that admin. I was very glad I asked, as I would have never thought about asking that one simple question, nor could I have anticipated the powerful response.

That example had a positive resolution, but that doesn't always happen. What happens if you don't ask or take advice? I have a great example of a time I did this, and the inevitable consequences. Once, I was managing a team, and we occasionally ran to the courthouse to collect records. I remember one particular investigator on that team. He was young, just out of college, and he served as a law enforcement explorer, then later as a volunteer, for a police department. Law enforcement explorers are career programs for young adults to gain practical experience in various law enforcement careers. This candidate was confident and self-assured. All good qualities, but his people skills were a bit challenged.

One day I had a simple task for him. I asked him to go to the courthouse to conduct some research and retrieve records for a complex case I was working on. Before he went, I told him we would need to review the process when asking the clerk for assistance. His response was pretty negative. He said he "knew what to do" and that you "just ask for the records and they give them to you." I told him it really wasn't that simple—that there was an "art" to the way you ask for assistance. I explained it is important to approach the clerk in a way that is friendly and is very respective of their time. I explained that these clerks get hundreds of requests, and most folks are not considerate of their time, so being very sympathetic in your approach can go a long way. I also gave the following advice: first, if there is a line and you need to wait, just stand quietly, no matter how long it takes, and don't complain. Next, when you reach the window, start with a big smile, ask how the clerk how their day is going, and let them know you are not familiar with their system. Tell them it is your first time researching, and you're a bit confused. Let them know you'd appreciate any assistance they could provide. I laughed and added that it would be a nice touch to take flowers with you, but no matter what, to be friendly and kind in your approach.

He returned a couple hours later. The first thing he said was, "You were so right!" He went on to explain there were a couple of guys in front of him who were not so polite to the clerk, so she responded in the same manner, and the conversations did not go well. Needless to say, that group did not end up with the information they were looking for. When it was his turn, he decided to take my advice, and to his surprise, it worked perfectly. He said he really didn't believe what I told him until he watched the two people in front of him fail miserably. At the end of the day, it really was a simple thought process, with a powerful lesson that translates to many aspects of investigations: put yourself in someone else's shoes. Various situations should be always be observed and analyzed to determine the best approach when dealing with people.

Similarly, careful thought should also go into surveillance planning. Proper surveillance technique is a lesson in adaptability. I once faced a challenge in determining how to best approach a surveillance project. You can read about my dilemma, and decide how you would approach the project. You will see how adaptable an investigator needs to be in order to get the best results for their client.

In this case, I had a client claim a company had product in a warehouse, and they wanted me to provide them with proof. My first thought was to conduct surveillance, spending a few hours with some binoculars, and I would find what I needed. However, I quickly learned the facility in question was located on a small alley with the only parking located directly across from the bay door, which was the surveillance vantage point: a bay door. I had to look around for an inconspicuous location, where I could blend in. The challenge was that I needed to see inside the bay door, and to do so, I needed to be right in front of the office, next to that bay door. That position would not be a clandestine location for undercover work. Luckily the traffic was not heavy, with very few vehicles going to other companies. The dilemma facing me, was how would I sit in plain sight, for hours, waiting for a glimpse inside that warehouse? This type of situation could be altered for just about any stationary surveillance. However, this surveillance was unique in that it ended with a surprise.

I started out by parking across the alley, facing the company. I sat there for about 20 minutes, watching the activity. There were various vehicles and trucks, but not a lot of thru traffic. No one was walking or lingering outside the warehouses. It actually seemed unusually quiet, and the lack of activity made it difficult to blend in. Blending in is very important. When conducting a stationary surveillance, you don't want to be that one person who stands out from everyone else. As I looked across to the business I was tasked with observing, I noticed a glass door entrance to the office. On the other side of that door could be a waiting room, or a receptionist.

I really had no idea. If this company had a receptionist, she could be looking right at me, wondering what I was doing. As I sat there, my mind worked overtime, wondering what story I would have if someone came outside and asked what I was doing. I have had people come up to me a few times, and sometimes they will just call the police. In any event, it is always important to have a believable story ready to provide to them. In this case, my standard stories would not work very well. Unfortunately, due to the location, I was too far from the main road to use the "my car broke down" excuse, and it wasn't really a location where I could say "I'm waiting for a friend." So I racked my brain, and finally, it came to me. An excuse I could use that was believable. Luckily I had the props available to pull it off.

Most investigators have various props, which are objects for use in a performance, handy in their vehicles for various situations they may face. Examples include different hats, jackets, photographs, things to hang on the rear-view mirror—all to help change their appearance and support their story during a stationary or moving surveillance. I opened up my glove box and was happy to find my one prop which assisted me on several surveillances. It was an old picture of my oldest daughter. It was not the best quality picture, but it would do. I smiled for a moment and got out of my car.

Before I went back outside, I made sure to also determine my pretext, or my cover story. For those of you not familiar with the term *pretext*, generally it is a reason or story given to cover up the real story or reason. One important thing to remember when you come up with a pretext is to make sure to keep it simple and as close to the truth as possible. It makes it easier to remember and think quickly if things get a bit sticky. I gave it some thought, and I knew exactly what I would do.

It was show time. I walked right up to that glass door and went inside. I was right, there was a young woman sitting at her desk who greeted me with a smile. I immediately smiled back and introduced myself. She asked how she could assist me. I put on my concerned face and began my story. I told her that my niece had run away from home recently and we knew she was dating a young man, who was several years older than her. He was a delivery man and we heard she would ride with him sometimes to his deliveries. It was my understanding that he worked a few offices down and I was hoping to find her with him. I pointed to my car and told her I would be parking across the way watching for them. I let her know that I was from out of town and in a car she wouldn't recognize. I let her know I came into the office because I didn't want her to be alarmed that I would be parking there for at least a day or so. The young lady asked a few questions about my niece, how long she had been gone and if I had a picture of her. I showed her the picture and we talked about teenagers and the changes they go through at that age. I thanked her for her time and went back to my car. I sat there for a couple of hours, but, to my dismay, there was no activity and not once did anyone open the bay door to the warehouse. Little did I know, my story would yield more fringe benefits than I had ever imagined.

The next day I returned, around mid-morning. After about an hour the young lady I spoke with the previous day came out and walked over to my car. She was smiling as she walked towards me, so I knew things were good. I opened my window and we greeted one another. She said she informed her boss about my niece, and he felt bad about my situation, and asked her to invite me to have lunch at their office. Without hesitation, I accepted.

I used this amazing opportunity to further my investigation. Her boss greeted me as I walked into their conference room where I was surprised to see a nice lunch spread out on the table. He invited me to make a sandwich. He began to tell me a story about his daughter who ran away from home when she was young. We chatted for about 20 minutes, then I let him know I should get back to my car. As I was walking out, I asked the young lady if I could use the restroom, which happened to be located right by an open door to the warehouse. I noticed a soda machine in the warehouse. This was another opportunity. When I came out, I asked if I could get a soda from the machine that was in the warehouse. She said it was no problem and walked with me to the machine. I asked about their business and showed interest by asking questions. This led to her offering to show me the warehouse, which was an amazing benefit to my case. Now I could examine it for the benefit of my client, right under their noses, with their consent!

Ultimately, my pretext was extremely beneficial to my case. Because of it, I had lunch with the owner of the company I was investigating, a tour of their warehouse, plus I was able to verify the company did not have the product they shouldn't have had. This was a good day. My client was happy and so was I. This was a good outcome, as I would have hated to see those folks in trouble after being so nice about the situation with my "niece."

This chapter talked a lot about basic investigations. This is where it all starts; from the basics. It's a foundation upon which all future investigations will be based. Starting out with high expectations is a terrific approach, but always remember to be adaptable in whatever you do. Consider the future of your work and the knowledgebase necessary to remain relevant. Our world is constantly changing and technology is your future. There is something new to learn every day, and you should embrace this fact. I have been in this field close to 40 years and I continue to learn and adapt myself to the changes that guide me to the next level. Investigations are dynamic and complex. It is critical to get out and talk to people, understand technology, listen, and look into the future to see what's new. Soon you will be immersed in technology. The millennium children will be working and they grew up with technology. The Internet of Things will be embedded into everyday life, and you will be investigating technology. Adapt to it, don't fear it.

Note

1. Source: Eyiaro, Bunmi. "Definitions: Adaptability." Available at: https://teenafrica academy.org/demo/news/.

Chapter 10

Confidence

Bill Majeski

I have been in the investigative field for 50 years and I have conducted tens of thousands of interviews and interrogations. I offer this chapter as a guide to anyone who wants to be the best possible professional investigator. I will focus on the importance of confidence as an important attribute of a great investigator, drawing upon my experience as a detective, a polygraph expert, and a licensed private investigator.

First, I would like to start by providing my definition of investigation. In its most basic form, an investigation is an effort by an individual or group to unravel convoluted information, find answers to intricate questions, ascertain facts and solve a mystery. When we factor in the numerous forensic developments and technological advances, we come to recognize the necessity for specializations. Investigative experts are deemed essential in the furtherance of many investigations. Such experts include crime scene investigators, DNA profilers, forensic accountants, toxicologists, linguistics experts, dark web mavens, data recovery gurus, and polygraph experts. Next, confidence. The definition of confidence is "a feeling or consciousness of one's powers or of reliance on one's circumstances."[1]

The primary investigator on a given case is the one who determines the need and orchestrates the use of any outside experts during their investigative process. Their knowledge, skill and experience give them the authority to analyze, evaluate and apply their expertise to a broad range of decisions, all in the advancement of their investigation. Private Investigators, or PIs are indeed experts in their broad-based discipline of investigations.

One example of such expertise is polygraph examination. I had the privilege, along with two eminently qualified colleagues, of operating a polygraph school in New York City for about ten years. I will share some of that experience with you. Here, you will see that this is a field where confidence is a critical element to the success of the examiner.

The Polygraph is a device that measures a subject's physical response to the questions asked of them. Working in the area of polygraphs is a profession unlike any other in the field of investigation. It is unique. There are only a few thousand qualified examiners who are inter-dispersed throughout local, state, and federal law enforcement agencies and corporate investigative departments throughout the country. And, of course, there are private examiners, many of whom are retired from law enforcement, and others who worked their way into a challenging career.

Working as a polygraph examiner is a demanding career, but the one qualifying characteristic that is essential in making a good examiner is a high degree of self-confidence. The polygraph examiner stands as the sole arbiter in determining truth or deception which, in many instances, decrees innocence or guilt. The consequences are huge. In law enforcement, a polygraph examination represents the gateway for an accused to either go home or go to trial, in the corporate sector it could mean keeping the job or being let go, and in the private arena, staying together or getting a divorce.

The polygraph examiner must have the confidence to work independently. Unlike other types of professional investigators, who are free to seek assistance from others, the polygraph examiner works alone. From beginning to end, a polygraph examiners' investigative process is completed in less than a few hours when an expected judgment is made based on their interpretations.

The polygraph examiner must also be confident in their decisions. To be sure, confidence is essential in all good investigators, especially in uniformed officers, who are too often called upon to make life or death decisions. But polygraph examiners, especially in law enforcement are required to make decisive decisions on every test they conduct, in many instances, daily. Additionally, for polygraph examiners, there is often a mandate to proceed to an interrogation after an examinee reveals deception. There is no room for error here. Making the wrong call will not only damage the psyche of any good examiner, but it could alter the direction of a criminal investigation. New investigators should not be daunted by this news. When you make hard decisions frequently, this process will greatly enhance your individual confidence level and will serve to bolster your confidence and assist with future decision making.

The classes I taught were aimed at former law enforcement, former military and civilians. The course work was multifaceted and demanding but the only common concern among all students was fear about making the correct decisions when calling a subject truthful or deceptive.

Fear is a powerful obstacle, which can prevent a person from moving forward. In investigations, it is often predicated on the anticipation that your decision might or will be wrong. Diagnosing this fear of drawing a conclusion will help to identify any deficiencies in your investigative process, or in the case of an examiner, any deficiencies in proper polygraph procedures, especially the question formulation segment.

Here, confidence is key. Fear in investigative decision making is most often caused by self-doubt. This lack of confidence can be greatly diminished or eliminated when concerted effort is taken in building your investigation. If you determine that you followed your prescribed methodology, your conclusion will most often be correct. Defining the problem, creating the framework, proper and complete research, information collection, analysis of data, follow-ups, and conclusions, all of these will lead to a confident decision. Think of confidence as you would a muscle; the more often it is exercised, the stronger it will be.

Strong communication skills are essential for any investigator and will serve to boost confidence. Communication in the field of investigations is both an art and a science. Every investigation requires the exchange of information, most often in the form of interviewing. The competence of any investigator to express a message and positively interact with others is central to a good investigative process. It's a critical component in one's methodology that will allow for productive information which most often leads to successful results. The development of respectable communication skills is required of any good investigator. This act of conveying and receiving information verbally and sending and receiving messages non-verbally is a multi-layered process.

Strong communication skills are pivotal during the interview process. In terms of the spoken word, as an investigator conveying and receiving information, there are several principal elements which, if followed, will secure a greater level of self-confidence during any conversation, especially interviews.

In order to enhance the communication process, investigators are encouraged to exercise positive self-talk. Self-talk is a form of internal conversation where you can improve your feelings and behavior by using positive, rather than negative, messaging. For instance, when it rains, positive thinking would focus on the fact that you have an umbrella handy, rather than focusing on the fact it will be a grey, cloudy day. This technique can be very helpful and effective when used by investigators before communicating with their subjects.

Why? Exercising positive self-talk in investigations, such as convincing yourself that the interview will go well, will help facilitate positive outcomes. It is an easy way to positively influence any situation. It is also a great exercise to help boost your confidence in interview settings. After all, if you cannot convince yourself to have a good experience in a given interview setting, it will be challenging to convince others to talk with you about potentially uncomfortable topics.

It is also a good idea to employ relaxation techniques during interviews, undercover operations, and other critical situations. Anxiety can draw blood flow away from the brain, in a fight or flight response, and slow down cognitive function. Deep breathing will help in these situations to relax and bring in more oxygen.

Confidence in the subject matter can also serve to reduce anxiety. Know your subject matter before any meeting and be prepared with questions, or, at a minimum, have the information necessary to make quick, informed decisions. When you are well informed about your case, this information will allow you to better control the conversations you have in an interview setting. Confidence in your subject matter will enable you to be confident in the investigative process. Thinking and speaking clearly to your subject, and listening very carefully to every response will allow for the best flow of information. It is important to remember that most people hear what is being said, but good investigators must listen to evaluate what is being said.

Non-verbal communication, such as body language, is also a critical part of any interview. Most experts agree that non-verbal communication represents at least 60% of all communication. Investigators must have the ability to send and receive silent messages and evaluate non-verbal responses. There are several principal elements which, if followed, will secure a greater level of self-confidence during any conversation, especially interviews. Investigators should always sit or stand straight and dress professionally, which projects confidence. It is important to remember the person you are speaking with is either consciously or unconsciously evaluating you and making their own judgment about you. The initial impression that you portray during an interview can easily tilt the progress either in your favor, or against you. Any image of perceived weakness will welcome at best disinterest, at worst, defiance. It is important to be mindful of the subject's non-verbal reactions as you are asking questions, and while they are responding. Be aware of your own facial expressions and physical reactions throughout the conversation.

My Experience

After spending more than 20 years as a Detective in the New York City Police Department (NYPD) then 30 years, and going strong, involved in the profession of Private Investigations, I would be remiss if I did not mention some differences and similarities. The Badge, comes with a grant of formal governmental authority. Although it opens many doors, it closes others.

Let me give you an example of how being confident can lead to positive investigative outcomes. Here, you will see how two very different investigative approaches can yield varying results. In 1969, when I was a young, inexperienced detective, I was sent to Florida, which was over 1000 miles outside of my jurisdiction to locate and interview two people. These witnesses were needed to confirm testimony that would be given at trial in a politically explosive case. After exhaustive research, the only information available on the witnesses was a former work location for one of them, a nightclub/bar in Florida. Going into a bar in New York City to get information would have been seamless; this would not be the case in Coconut Grove.

Usually, licensed establishments cooperate with the police, so I found the owner and identified myself as a NYPD Detective. Before I could begin to explain why I was there and who I was looking for, this bar owner became outright hostile. He loudly questioned my authority in the State of Florida adding that he had no use for cops and liked NY cops even less. Clearly, I was not welcome. In retrospect, I realize my timing was bad. In the late 1960s, Coconut Grove flourished as the seat of South Florida's Bohemian life. Clearly my suit and tie made me stand out as a beacon of the establishment, in an anti-establishment environment.

After being dismissed and asked to leave the premises, I went back to my motel and thought about what happened, and what I could have done to change that outcome. I quickly realized that governmental authority sometimes has very little authority. My confidence had been bruised, but I was not deterred. I decided I simply could not go back to New York without the crucial information.

I decided to return that evening and take a different approach; one where I exuded confidence. This time, I wore laid-back attire that allowed me to "blend-in" with my surroundings. I also included a pair of pilot sunglasses, and a relaxed attitude. I placed myself at the bar, far away from the office of the owner, where I had my first negative encounter. I proceeded to order a drink, like any other patron. After my second drink, I over-tipped the bartender and asked if he could possibly help me. My story was short and to the point; I told him I was trying to find my cousin "Lenny" (my witness, who once worked at this bar) because his father was very sick, and his mother did not know how to get in touch with him. So basically, I said his mother asked me to help her, and therefore I needed his help, in order to help her. Asking for "help" is a winning approach in investigative interviewing, to get the information you seek. People love to "help" others and will often jump at the chance to do so. Case in point, my bartender. Not sure he followed the story, but it was good enough to get me a current address for the witness, in Miami. I left another tip, thanked him for his much-needed help, and made a point of calling out and waving to the owner as I exited the front door. Outside I smiled broadly and felt the exhilaration of regained confidence. I'd had a lot of trepidation about going back to the bar that evening, but I felt uncomfortable losing confidence in myself, and I knew the longer I waited, the more difficult it would be. I also realized that advanced planning was critical to my successful approach.

Private sector investigations offer a different set of challenges. The PI License carries with it many of the same moral responsibilities as public service, with fewer benefits, and fewer limitations. Access to official records are constrained, people are less inviting, as they view the profession as more self-serving, and there is no longer a psychological force of having the criminal justice system on your side. Conversely, police rules and procedures are rigid as opposed to being self-imposed and many of the investigations do not entail complex prosecutions. In policework, there are many options. Here, the investigative work is incredibly diverse and there are opportunities to specialize and work on preferred cases, there are many resources available to assist the investigator, and the freedom of investigative creativity is limited only by one's imagination and self-confidence.

The police officers who chose to become PIs are often falsely led by their confidence to believe it will be a seamless career transition. In my experience in the field of private investigations, the business failure rate seems to be higher than average. Nationally, 20 percent of new businesses fail within the first year; 50 percent within five years.[2] Yet upon retirement there have been countless police officers that have "hung out their shingle," deciding to parlay their investigative background into a career as a PI. Why do they do it? I think it is due to their inherent confidence. Police officers are by their very nature confident about performing their duties. However, confidence exhibits itself in many different forms and under many different conditions. Being confident making a car stop, interceding in a household dispute, confronting a disorderly group, disrupting a robbery, fighting a fleeing felon, and numerous other acts of selfless dedication do not necessarily set the stage for the transition into the profession of a Private Investigator. As a law enforcement officer personal independence is, in most instances, severely limited, conformity to procedures and rules of conduct are the order of the day, every day. Most law enforcement retirees that transition into investigations ultimately find a comfortable fit working for some enterprise or other governmental agency. Those who ultimately succeed in the PI profession brought with them their experience that shaped their confidence, but they also brought a strong belief in their ability to successfully traverse the challenges of running a business.

Overall, a successful private investigator must be confident in their ability to dominate several skill areas at once in order to have a successful business. The best PIs must be able to find the clients, convince them that they can accomplish the client's goals and complete the assignments, achieve the necessary results, and at the same time deal with the exhaustive perseverance of running a business. PI's have a strong trust in their own abilities, believe that they can conquer any fears, blaze a trail to their destiny, with realistic expectations, while striving to maintain a positive mindset.

Case Study

I would like to present a case study of how I used confidence to solve a major case as a PI. Throughout this case study, I will provide useful tips on how to prepare a case for investigation. The case I will discuss was one of my first complex projects as a new PI. I received this matter through a law firm that represented a major corporation that was embroiled in a multi-layered lawsuit. The case involved a large Superfund site. A Superfund is an Environmental Protection Agency (EPA) program tasked with cleaning up contaminated land. This one was located in a small town in the Southeast United States.

This first step in any investigative case is intake. In this case, it meant conducting a careful review of the available documentation. With this case, the initial impact to me was the large volume of material that was sent to my home office for review and analysis. I received seven legal boxes of documentation, including court fillings, corporate documents, maps and assorted notes. Knowing that I only had the weekend to get back to them with my recommendations put me into a bit of a panic. I am dyslexic, so reviewing large volumes of written material can be especially challenging. I knew I could never get through the material in a timely manner, so I had to think quickly, and improvise.

How did I tackle this case? Carefully and methodically. I knew I had to be thoughtful in my approach. Unraveling complex cases is a daunting task and should be probed thoughtfully. I previously worked on large-scale investigations in the police department, where mistakes were made, and lessons were learned. This experience allowed me to approach the depth of this assignment with caution, but without concern. I knew I had to make the material digestible, but I didn't have to be an expert in the case from the beginning. You have to start somewhere.

If you find yourself in this position, positive affirmation can help. Sometimes, closing your eyes, taking a deep breath and just telling yourself that "you can do this" is empowering. Approaching any undertaking, especially those cases that include an abundance of material should be first viewed thoughtfully. Identify the problem (your case assignment), think about solutions (your approach), solve them (your results).

This is what I did. To begin, I spent hours organizing the material into manageable, logical piles. Next, I scanned the material to gain a good understanding of what each stack represented. I gave a heading to each pile, which included comments, questions and possible measures that could be undertaken to develop each area. By Monday's conference call, I was prepared enough to speak intelligently about the matter, demonstrating I was prepared to move forward with the project.

During the call, I was certain to practice thoughtful listening. Having written notes, reviewing them and separating them for easy access prior to a conference call does stabilizes one's self-assurance. Equally important is listening intently. This conference call included the senior litigator, two associate attorneys and a paralegal, all of whose names were jotted down immediately and used in my dialogue to them. Listening intently for key points during the conversation and quickly referencing notes allowed me to engage informatively.

My confidence allowed me to recognize my limitations. Yet I didn't let them stop me from succeeding. I was immediately overwhelmed at the sheer volume of the material, but I quickly found a way to make it more manageable. One might think a confident investigator would assume they could master the material without much review. However, that is not always the best approach. A confident investigator knows it is important to make sure they understand the case at hand and conduct a careful evaluation to make sure it is the right case for them and their experience and background before accepting the engagement. Being confident that you could investigate any type case, under any circumstances is a great attitude to have but, being wrong could come at a great personal cost.

A confident investigator also knows it is important to ask for an expert to assist, when needed. Any good investigator follows their own established process, but when confronted with an unfamiliar type of assignment they know their confidence level will be better served after consulting with others who have different skill-sets and can best inform their investigative steps. In this investigation, the law firm had already engaged environmental and engineering experts, all of who were available for consultations. Their explanations of technical matters gave me a clear understanding and allowed me to formulate relevant questions during my interviews.

Preparation is a critical part of any investigation. Careful case preparation will give you confidence in your investigative abilities. There is a direct correlation between the level of a successful conclusion to an investigation and the effort expended on the preparation for each phase of that investigation. You can do one without the other, but it would be like jumping out of an airplane without knowing how to open the reserve parachute. Preparation in all things will give you the confidence to trust yourself and the decisions you make while working on the case.

As a key part of their preparations, investigators should create an "image" of what the case "looks like." In other words, develop a road map for your investigative process. In this case, keen preparations gave me an understanding of the complex material, which allowed for the development of a hypothesis, questions to establish clarity and a list of proposed actions for consideration, all of which were written out for use during the phone conference the next morning.

Every short-term goal was accomplished during the conference call. That was the easy part. The initial stage of the actionable investigation was reviewing the documents for potential targets. Ultimately, the targets would be the people in that sleepy town who might best help me develop the necessary information to determine who was at fault.

This is what I learned from the documents. Initially, a Superfund site, a polluted/contaminated area, was discovered as a result of over two dozen cancer cases clustered in a small area of homes. It was determined each of these patients utilized local well water. It was discovered that toxins saturated the soil at a manufacturing facility, not far from the homes, and were carried through underground water affecting the homes' water wells. The manufacturing plant had been closed for two and a half years and had gone through three ownership changes since our client company sold it 28 years before.

Our client created the facility and owned it for the longest period. They built and operated it for about 15 years before selling it to another company. Each subsequent company manufactured similar products, and each utilized the same basic process. The second company operated there for about 12 years, before selling to the third owner who owned it for another ten years. Finally, it was sold to the fourth and final owner, who went out of business after four years, when the first of the cancer-related law suits began. The facility had since been abandoned.

The next step would be for me to find my targets. I knew from my research there would be many obstacles in my search process. It was important for me to identify those obstacles upfront and determine the best way to tackle them ahead of time.

For instance, in this case, there were several challenges. For one, I knew that my targets would likely have very mixed emotions about this case. Many people in the town relied on the manufacturing plant either directly or indirectly for economic survival. Additionally, many people were negatively affected, either directly or indirectly, from the cancer cases being diagnosed. The association between the plant and the cancer cases created emotional complexities among the town's residents. As such, it was critically important for the investigator in this case to recognize those complexities and be understanding and empathetic to the situation.

The next separate, but related, challenge was finding witnesses/targets who could provide testimony and help to unravel the mysteries involved in the toxic dumping and massive cover-up. My desire to seek justice in this case drove me to pursue all possible leads. My efforts were ultimately worthwhile. Everyone I interviewed who was involved with the plant had some viable information.

Another challenge in this case was my status as a new PI. Although I had considerable investigative experience, the world of private investigations was different. I had not worked on cases such as this in the past. I also was working outside my comfort zone in terms of location. I was in an area where I didn't know anyone and that was culturally very different from home. I initially didn't feel comfortable. Any investigator who is working private cases will ultimately find themselves in this situation.

In this case, confidence is key. It was important for me to control the conversation. It is harder for people to relay information to someone that appears nervous, overly apologetic, is fumbling or just generally seems unsure of themselves. Self-confidence in your approach, demeanor, verbal dialogue and non-verbal behavior will demand the attention of the recipient.

It is also challenging to convince people to testify in court. Often the attorneys in the case will bear this responsibility. However, if you are skilled enough to tackle the logistics of orchestrating witnesses, your skill will be appreciated and your status as an investigator will be elevated.

I quickly learned the people who had information about the case would not be easy to reach. It turned out that targets had been previously identified, but no actions were taken. The law firm had already made failed attempts at gaining any form of cooperation from the people that I had selected from the documents. The targets had either had moved out of town, passed on, were too old to care about the case, or didn't trust the "Big City" law firm. It was clear that I would need to "tone down" any traits that might "out" me as a New Yorker to win over these targets.

I was not deterred and decided to try my luck at gaining their cooperation. Keep in mind, back then, this meant quite a lot of work. The World Wide Web had not yet been invented, so searching for people was a completely different process then it is today. Pre-internet, in rural areas, it was common to go on location, knock on doors and have face-to-face conversations as a fact-finding mission when looking for people. It was an effective way of developing further information, which remains effective to this day (and is often the preferred method of furthering an investigation).

I embarked on my mission. I knew this would not be easy. I would have to muster every bit of confidence I had in order to convince this group of people to talk to me. I decided the best investigative technique was for me to assimilate. I needed to really get to know the local area, its places and people.

After checking into the closest motel, about 15 miles outside of town, I spent the next five days hanging out at the local coffee shop and family restaurant by day, and the local tavern by night. After three and a half days of countless conversations, mostly about nothing important, one person showed a willingness to have a meaningful conversation about the closed plant. That conversation led to introductions to other friends and neighbors. This process is called "snowball sampling," wherein you recruit additional participants by asking the ones you have, for additional people who could help you. Sometimes this is the only way to obtain additional witnesses in a given case. Phrasing the request in such a way as soliciting "help" rather than information is also a wise investigative technique. People always want to help others—it is part of their human nature. But give information? This sounds a little more threatening.

Word started getting around, and my list of targets was growing. Back in New York we now had four individuals who could potentially be helpful to our fact-finding mission. Over the next eight months I located and interviewed over 50 people, mostly former employees, and gathered 21 affidavits attesting to the toxic dumping activities at the plant that took place under each of its ownerships.

Each interview I conducted in the case had value—the subject either provided a new clue or put me in contact with another person. In one instance, an interviewee offered the identities of three people who were present when a garage and storage shed were built over a large trench that was used for dumping toxic waste. Each interview helped to re-create a picture of events as they progressed over the years and which actions occurred when each of the corporate owners controlled the facility.

The next phase of my work involved determining which of the many potential witnesses would best be suited to establish culpability of the various corporate entities involved in the contamination of the property. The law firm I was working for was only involved with the liability for the Superfund site and its clean-up. Utilizing my notes and my perceptions of each of the potential witnesses, a series of long meetings were held at the law firm to establish a priority list of potential witnesses. They were valued based on their first-hand knowledge of the events as they occurred over the years. Their testimony would be aimed at lending support to the environmental evidence and help identify a timeline as to what events took place. There was no doubt as to the damage to local water supplies and land contamination. What needed more clarity was the philosophy of management in the various organizations that ran the facilities, the knowledge of the potential dangers, the due diligence or lack thereof and participation of specific individuals. All of this information was necessary in establishing responsibility and liability.

I had a hard time finding witnesses who would come to New York City. You would think a free trip there for a few days would entice a long list of volunteers. Unfortunately, many of the potential witnesses had little or no interest in participating in any litigation, irrespective to where that testimony would be given. Some individuals completely refused to participate in any depositions. Fortunately there were an adequate number of witnesses who were willing to appear. Their testimony strongly supported the environmental evidence which was provided by several eminently qualified environmental experts.

The final settlement for the environmental damage had all the previous owners paying disproportionate amounts into a Superfund, which would be used to remove contaminants and help repair and restore the local environment. Their total contributions saved the taxpayers many millions of dollars.

Final Thought

Becoming a good Private Investigator does not happen overnight; however, if it is a profession you have a desire to pursue, then you already possess some fundamental qualities that will serve you well in your quest. Consider the reasons that you personally believe you can be an investigator, examine them, then justify them to yourself. If you can do this, then you have laid the beginnings of a foundation upon which you can begin building your career. You have established your first layer of self-confidence.

Notes

1. Merriam-Webster Dictionary.
2. www.investopedia.com/slide-show/top-6-reasons-new-businesses-fail/.

Chapter 11

Creativity

Charles-Eric Gordon

Most often, people associate creativity with the performing arts, fine arts and the humanities. Many would not consider that creativity can be used in other professional fields and endeavors such as engineering, science and business. Surprisingly, many would not consciously associate creativity with investigative work.

Creativity does in fact, and often, assist in solving investigative problems and what appears, at first glance, to be a dead end. Virtually no investigator, either in law enforcement or in the private sector will be successful if this creativity is not present.

I have a recent example of creativity being used by an investigator. Detective Paul Holes of the Contra Costa County District Attorney's Office in California uploaded a DNA sample from a 1980's homicide to a genealogy website in early 2018. With the assistance of genealogists, it was possible to identify the perpetrator, known as the Golden State Killer through the DNA test results posted online by his relatives.

In order to demystify the concept of creativity, I offer the following alternate words for consideration. These words include, but are not limited to; innovation, resourcefulness and imagination. In its simplest terms, creativity might be defined as "thinking outside of the box."

Creativity is not necessarily inherent. Some researchers believe that it can be acquired by nature, rather than nurture. Yet many believe that creativity is not just a natural talent or gift, but a quality that can be developed and enhanced through study, mindful observation, and most of all, practice.

Now that we have defined what creativity is, let's examine what creativity does. Creativity in the investigative field enables the investigator to seek out and develop new and valuable solutions, or at least improvements, in problem solving. Furthermore, it requires the professional investigator to identify problems or issues that need to be dealt with. Persistence in the development of "work arounds," or methods for solving problems, is very important.

The use of creativity in investigations includes "off label" uses of solutions that have worked in other fields, such as psychology, sales, and negotiations. As will be discussed later, it is extremely important for investigators to be curious and well-rounded in several fields, informed by their reading, television viewing habits and general outlook. Creativity is fueled by both formal and informal education.

How Creativity can be Developed and Enhanced

Investigators can increase their creative abilities in several ways, which will also be beneficial when "off duty." It is highly recommended that investigators sharpen their creativity skills by developing a broad base of knowledge. Creative investigators are life-long learners who live a curiosity-driven life. Investigators who wish to develop their knowledge base will take courses in Criminal Justice and similar specialized disciplines, yet also enroll in courses in sociology, geography, literature, art, and creative writing. Classes in drama and acting can also be invaluable for those who wish to perfect their skills as an undercover operative.

Investigators will often derive creative benefits from leisure activities. Having hobbies, observing people, solving different types of puzzles, hiking and taking walks will sharpen an investigator's mind and powers of observation making it more receptive to creative thinking. Listening to music, looking at painting and photographs will hone one's skills of observation. Oftentimes, sudden flashes of insight occur when your mind is involved with something else.

Investigators should also strive to be well-read. Investigators who read widely, including at least one major newspaper, will have the information they need to be more creative. Reading fiction can spark creativity, especially detective and espionage novels. Biographies of Allan Pinkerton, William Burns and other legendary detectives may also sharpen one's creativity. Reading and enjoying Sherlock Holmes stories written by Sir Arthur Conan Doyle, about the legendary detective imbued with extraordinary creativity along with his skills of deductive and inductive reasoning will reveal his "out of the box" thinking in the investigative profession.

It is important to always have a way of jotting down ideas (pen and paper or your smartphone) as you never know when a sudden inspiration may occur. It can happen when waking from a dream, doing the dishes, shaving, listening to music, or watching heavy rain or a snowstorm. Remember, creative solutions often enter your consciousness when you are not consciously trying to solve a case.

Observing children can also spark creative ideas. Simply watching the creativity exhibited by children as they play using repurposed objects (not store-bought toys) such as kitchen pots, pans, utensils, scraps of building materials and large boxes and crates, can stimulate your own creativity. Children are the kings and queens of imagination and creativity.

My Background: Education and Experience as an Investigator

My Creative Youth

I was always a creative person. As a child, I was always drawing with crayons, both in coloring books, but, more often, pictures and designs of my own. I loved using the different colors, especially in some offbeat combinations. I also loved mosaic tile kits and other arts and craft activities. As I got older, I enjoyed creative writing and wrote mediocre poetry.

Some of my most creative activities happened at my grandparents' Brooklyn apartment. There, with the exception of some old deflated rubber balls, from my father and his siblings' childhood, no toys were available. However, my brother, cousins and I discovered ways to entertain ourselves—by playing with my grandfather's incomplete decks of pinochle cards, clothespins and small objects that he brought home from the children's underwear factory, where he was a partner. My cousin taught me how to create missiles using these items.

My most favorite creative activity at my grandparents' home was reading the telephone directories. These are in short supply today. For reference, they were printed books that contained telephone numbers for local businesses and people. In these books, I spent hours looking for interesting or humorous names, and learning the colorful telephone exchanges that existed in Brooklyn years ago. The first two digits were the first two letters of descriptive names, such as Hyacinth, Ingersol, Cloverdale, President and Nightingale. These numbers would often reappear in the "phone books" that I would compose as a child.

Overall, I was never bored for very long. I used whatever was available at the time to keep me occupied and engaged. This is an important facet of creativity.

I have been involved in various facets of the investigative field for over 40 years. I graduated from State University of New York (SUNY) Cortland with a major in English and minor in History. I began working as a debt collector for a major commercial bank in New York City where I began to the learn the art of "skiptracing" which entails tracking down debtors who have "skipped" out of their loans, credit card debts or other financial obligations.

Skiptracing is an art in the truest sense, as there are very few rules governing it. There are federal and state governmental laws and regulations on what actions are prohibited. The artistic part of skiptracing involves using various resources and techniques to locate missing debtors as well as other absentees such as heirs, beneficiaries, shareholders, witnesses, criminals and other hard-to-locate people. Skiptracing subjects have generally been absent for an extended period of time, and little information is known about them.

The skiptracing part of my job was very interesting and gave me the opportunity to be creative. I used different names, personas and devised different pretexts, or cover stories, to find debtors. It should be noted that today, virtually all use of pretext to locate consumer debtors is now prohibited by the federal Fair Debt Collection Act, Gramm Leach Bliley Act and other federal and state laws. However, there are still creative methods by which debtors and other absentees can be located; e.g., resourceful use of proprietary databases, inquiries to old neighbors and business in the debtor's former neighborhoods.

Then I decided to go to law school. After a year of working at the commercial bank, I was accepted to Brooklyn Law School where I earned a Juris Doctor degree in 1979 and passed the bar exam that summer. My major areas of study at Brooklyn Law School were criminal and commercial law. One summer, during law school, I worked at the bank and set up a skiptracing operation that focused on collecting a portfolio of ancient student loans. Although I interviewed with a few local District Attorneys' offices, I began working over the next five years with law firms that specialized in debt collection. At one law firm I often had to trace missing debtors whom the process servers were unable to locate for service of summons and complaints.

I quickly developed a name for myself in the area of investigations. Oftentimes, while I was working for these law firms, my former classmates from Brooklyn Law School would ask me for assistance with locating missing defendants, witnesses, heirs and even clients they had lost contact with. By 1983, I decided to open my own law practice in Forest Hills, New York, where I concentrated on tracing absconded debtors, missing heirs and beneficiaries to estates, witnesses to accidents and execution of wills, mortgages, shareholders and other absentees.

I was exempt from having to obtain a Private Investigator License. The New York State General Business Law, Section 83, exempts licensed attorneys from having to obtain a private investigator license for investigations "in the regular practice of law" which basically means an investigation with a legal nexus. There are similar exceptions in virtually all other states and Canadian provinces. The legislators in enacting these statutes realized that, having studied law for at least three years and having passed a strenuous bar admission examination, attorneys were sufficiently knowledgeable about laws and ethics and conducting themselves in a professional manner, or they could face disciplinary action including disbarment.

I have been regularly practicing full time as "investigative counsel" (the title that the New York Secretary of State permits me to use to describe my practice). I am prohibited from using the term "private investigator". As a licensed attorney and "officer of the court" I perform the same work as a private investigator and sometimes have greater access to information.

The only time I was not practicing full time as investigative counsel was in 1986 and 1987 when I worked as a "Special Investigator/Attorney" for the New York City Parking Violations Bureau as it was recovering from an infamous corruption scandal. I was cross designated as "Special Deputy Assistant Corporation Counsel" and given subpoena power. After working in a bureaucracy though, I was very happy to return to my full-time practice, which is now located in Woodbury, New York on Long Island.

Applied Creativity in Investigations

Incidental to my practice, I maintain a large collections of metropolitan area telephone directories dating back over 60 years in most cases. Using backdated directories is one means by which I have been able to trace the moves and sometimes ascertain the deaths of telephone subscribers in cases requiring the tracing of heirs, shareholders and other long-term absentees. Unfortunately, many people today do not have Verizon or non-cable landline service and therefore they are not listed in telephone directories.

Other creative means by which I have traced missing people include using databases, which are not set up primarily for investigative use, such as Ancestry.com, a genealogical database more focused on kinship. I also read two major newspapers and several professional publications daily. Even though some articles may not pertain to any current investigation cases, they may have information that might assist me indirectly by providing fresh insight and ideas. Being well read in many areas is extremely useful to all investigators.

I also recommend that investigators become familiar with a few foreign languages and their cultures. It is very helpful to be able to converse, to some degree, with people from communities and ethnic groups that one might encounter in their day-to-day work. For example, I use my basic knowledge and vocabulary of Polish, Russian, Yiddish and Spanish in order to converse with individuals and put them at ease. Additionally, my knowledge of various cultures, religions, and ethnic groups has enabled me to build trust and show respect to clients and subjects. For instance, I know to remove my shoes in a Muslim household, and not to attempt shaking hands with Orthodox Jewish women.

It is also important to respect all people. I cannot stress enough the need to be polite and respectful to other people, including governmental clerks, potential informants and others that you may encounter. Being respectful will assist you in obtaining further assistance, information and insight during an investigation. Your respect will be noted by those with whom you interact and will often elicit more information and cooperation.

It is also nice to provide a small gift to people who have assisted you. However, government employees are often unable to accept gifts due to laws governing this practice. Nevertheless, there are many creative ways to show appreciation for their assistance.

I have a few examples. For years, I received regular assistance from a clerk in a government office. We would regularly speak about food and cooking. A few times every summer and fall, I would provide her with my home-grown cayenne peppers that she enjoyed using in many of her recipes. A clerk in another governmental office who was very helpful to me needed some legal advice. I was more than happy to listen to her concerns and provide advice that enabled her to resolve the issue.

Bartering is a technique often employed by investigators. I have bartered information with investigators in both the public and private sectors, as long as this does not violate client confidentiality or laws against disclosure of classified or strictly confidential information. When you provide assistance to others in the field, they, in turn, will often assist you.

Other creative methods I have used that may be of value to other investigative professionals include the following.

- When testifying as an expert witness at a trial or other court proceeding, write your personal notes in shorthand, using obscure symbols or another alphabet. I have sometimes written out reference notes using the Cyrillic alphabet. If the opposing side demands to see what you are referring to, and the judge allows it, the notes will be of little value to the opposition.
- If you are preparing a highly confidential report, type it on an electric or manual typewriter. If you are using a computer, save your report on a separate flash drive. This will limit the risk of the report being wrongfully obtained through a computer hack. This creative solution is used by several foreign consulates in New York, most noteworthy the Russians, and, as a result, several years ago it led to a shortage and increase in prices for used IBM Selectric typewriters and other electronic typewriters.
- As stated before, read widely and take note of methods and techniques used in other occupations, professions and businesses that may be repurposed to solve cases or improve upon procedures that you use. Always keep an open mind both as an investigator and as an individual.
- Meet and interact with a wide cross-section of the population. You never know when you may learn something that will eventually, if not immediately, prove useful.
- Have interests outside of work. There are numerous ways to exhibit creativity as an investigator such as, pursuing "traditional creative" hobbies such as painting, sketching, writing, music and playing chess.
- Have a few cellphones, which are set up to block the outgoing number, all with different area codes. These can be used to both make unidentifiable calls or, if the circumstances of an investigation require it, the numbers from these various cellphones can be unblocked to facilitate contacting people who may be avoiding calls from your area code.
- Use these numbers as call back numbers. If the subject of a missing person investigation calls back, even if you do not answer and they do not leave a message (I suggest using the automated generic outgoing greeting), you may be able to trace the number through a proprietary or possibly even a free database.
- Devise the names of non-existent businesses with either neutral-sounding names, or reflecting specific types of business, areas of interest or ethnic backgrounds in order to have evasive individuals respond, displaying their phone number on your phone. Proprietary databases will often be able to match their phone number to a name, address, date of birth and, where permissible, a Social Security number.

- Consider setting up "dummy" corporations or doing business as (d/b/a) entities. These businesses are developed under a pseudonym and are different from the owner's registered, legal name. You can print a letterhead on your computer, utilizing a mail/receiving service such as UPS Plus, to receive mail. I have set up these entities in the past.

These are just a few creative techniques that may prove useful to investigators. Over time, with imagination and innovation, after listening to and learning from and adapting the "War Stories" of experienced professionals, you will develop other creative investigative methods.

Further Examples of Creativity from my Cases: Negotiations

An important recurring aspect of creativity in investigations, or in any other facet of human relations, is the art of negotiation. Negotiating is not a skill that one is born with, but is developed through life, through observation, study, and practice.

I have creatively utilized my negotiating skills over the years. I have often resolved challenges in obtaining information, and received cooperation from sources in the business and government sectors, as well as from individuals, where other investigative professionals have failed. How? By creatively crafting "win-win" solutions that benefit all parties. Using this technique, I was able to obtain the information that I needed, while my informants were able to assist me without violating privacy or other laws, confidentiality concerns, or their own principles.

There are many cases where investigators can be challenged to obtain necessary information and must exercise creativity. One type of case where this happens is rent regulation fraud investigations. In these cases, it is necessary to obtain as much proof as possible that the subject is not residing primarily in their rent-regulated apartment, and in fact has obtained a new legal and primary address. This is because a rent-regulated apartment is expected to be the tenant's primary residence. In order to qualify for rent-regulation, the tenant must be continually living in the apartment in question. Investigators might be hired to help a landlord prove otherwise.

To assist in these matters, investigators will need access to property records. In many states, drivers licensing, motor vehicle registration and voter registration information may be acquired through a Freedom of Information Law (FOIL) request. However, in some states, such information cannot be obtained with such a request.

Georgia is one such state. In the State of Georgia, driver or motor vehicle registration records cannot be obtained without the licensee or registrant's permission, or a court order from a Georgia judge. In one matter involving the

State of Georgia, I was able to reach the Deputy Commissioner of Legal Affairs for the Georgia Department of Motor Vehicles. Naturally, she was unable to violate her state's laws. However, due to the fact the information sought was to be used in a legal proceeding, I was able to create a "work around." On her Department's letterhead, and stamped with a state seal, she certified that the subject did, in fact, hold a Georgia driver's license. By not providing an address or other information and just confirming the person's name and date of birth that I provided, the Deputy Commissioner constructively complied with her state's statute, while providing me with the necessary information to prove that the subject was residing outside of the City of New York.

In a similar situation, I was able to obtain voter registration address and other information from counties in Pennsylvania. Typically, in this state, such records are only provided for election and law enforcement purposes. Yet I was able to convince the election officials that as an attorney at law, and officer of the court, this information was needed in a fraud investigation (albeit a civil one) and would only be used in connection with the investigation. I was permitted to submit the standard FOIL form, amended to include my explanation as to my purpose, and on similar occasions, my request was honored.

I was also able to creatively negotiate disclosure of information in compliance with applicable law in the UK. There, I was looking for a missing heir. The UK's Data Protection Law expressly prohibited the disclosure of a licensed driver's address to a third party, which was not a British law enforcement agency. Yet the supervisor that I spoke to by telephone was open-minded enough to assist me. She forwarded my contact information and the reason for my inquiry to the driver's license holder, who promptly contacted me himself!

I have used this technique many times since then. I will ask to have my information forwarded to heirs, beneficiaries and others whom I was trying to locate, when privacy considerations prohibit the disclosure of addresses and telephone numbers. This has been an effective negotiating tool that I have used with funeral homes, cemeteries, trade unions, college alumni associations and other non-government entities. It has also elicited help from former neighbors of missing individuals.

I have another example of how I creatively solved a case, with the use of intuition. I have always considered intuition to be a close relative of creativity and have, whenever possible, used it in working my cases. As you will see, recognizing one's intuitive thoughts can assist an investigator in solving a case.

In this case, I was looking for a distributee in a Surrogate's Court probate investigation. A distributee is an individual who would have been an heir, and inheriting from a decedent's estate, had the decedent died intestate, without having a valid will. If there is a valid will, relatives of various degrees of kinship are required by law to be notified of the probate of the will, under which they may not be inheriting what they would have received if there was no valid will. The courts generally require that a diligent effort must be made to locate and serve these distributees.

In this particular matter, the decedent's parents and grandparents had died before her, and she had no siblings, and thus no nephews or nieces. The closest relatives were first cousins and, if a first cousin had died, their children, if any, had to be notified of the decedent's death and the forthcoming petition to admit the decedent's will to probate.

As of this point, I had been unable to locate a death certificate or other acceptable proof of death for this missing cousin, whom other family members had not heard from for over 30 years. Since this investigation was conducted over 20 years ago, there were not yet open source websites or proprietary genealogical databases such as Ancestry.com. Instead, my research consisted of voter registration, drivers licensing and real property ownership files, and telephone directories. None of these sources provided any leads.

I was stymied in my efforts to find this cousin, until early the next day. In a half-awakened state early the next morning, the name "Saint Gertrude" came into focus in my drowsy mind. Not being a Catholic, I had very little knowledge of saints, beyond Saint Francis, Saint Joseph, Saint Michael and Saint Christopher.

What did Saint Gertrude have to do with this case? I visited a Catholic Bookstore a few days later and the helpful saleslady pulled a massive book from the shelf that listed each saint (and some names had numerous saints attached to them) their backgrounds, and whether they were patrons of any specific trade of classification of people. This book listed three or so 'Saint Gertrudes,' but nothing in their biographies shed any light on why I would, in my subconscious state, associate one of them with the missing cousin.

I had very little identifying information to work with in this case. Aside from this missing cousin's name and parents' names, approximate age, that she came from a Roman Catholic family, the only information that I had was her last known residence, over 30 years before, was on Long Island or Queens. No specific address was known. My intuition was some of the only concrete information I had in this case.

I trusted my intuition, and continued my research into Saint Gertrude. I returned to my large trove of telephone directories to search for any churches or other organizations under the name of Saint Gertrude. In short order, I was able to locate the cousin, who was put to rest in Saint Gertrude's R.C. Church cemetery. I was then able to obtain information from the church office and cemetery, including her date of death, age, last known address and the name and telephone number of a daughter who arranged for her funeral. The daughter provided me with her address and the names and addresses of her siblings. This allowed me to successfully complete my investigation, and the decedent's will was admitted to probate.

The foregoing is an example of why investigative professionals, and other people, should be receptive of intuitive thoughts that may occur to them, usually at unexpected times, while not actively working on the investigation.

Failure to be Creative

Unfortunately, some investigators are not innovative or creative thinkers. These individuals are often the ones working needlessly hard, and not necessarily obtaining results. They can often be seen "hammering away" at their computers; conducting the same database searches repeatedly, without regard to the special fact pattern or circumstances of the case at hand.

Investigative work, especially tracing missing persons, is an art and not a science. There are no "one size fits all" of "off the rack" solutions for every assignment or case. It is imperative that the investigator keep an open mind, and, if stymied, review the facts of the case, step away, do something enjoyable to unwind and then think about other ways to approach the matter.

Offbeat Methods that I have Used to Spark my Creativity

Constantly working from an office can be boring, and may stifle creative thought. The following are some techniques that I have used to stimulate creative thinking:

- In pleasant weather, I have often reviewed case files and conducted computer searches from the table in my backyard and at a picnic table in parks. I have even worked at the beach if I am not required to make telephone calls. (Just watch to make sure sand doesn't make its way into your iPad or laptop!)
- Working in front of a tropical fish tank may stimulate creativity.
- I often get creative ideas by watching the sprinklers water my lawn while I am on the patio in my backyard. Other investigators have confided that watching water helps their thought processes.
- Taking a break and drawing or sketching with colored pencils have provided a welcome time-out from a dead-end and has allowed me to approach the problem at hand with a fresh perspective.
- Taking notes and underlining materials with assorted pens, pencils and markers have helped me efficiently organize my notes, but added some fun and freshness when reviewing copies of documents, computer printouts, etc.

In Conclusion

As stated throughout this chapter, creativity is not some arcane activity that is only practiced in painters' studios, recording studios and at writers' workshops. Creativity occurs all around us and can be used for solving many different sorts of problems, including those encountered by investigators on a regular basis. Do not think that you have hit a dead end on a matter because "tried and true" methods that were previously successful failed to yield results. An innovative, open-minded approach may clear the case.

People who were not raised in an artistic, literary or musical environment can, with some effort, develop this valuable trait, regardless of their age. Being exposed to all varieties of mental stimuli, keeping a curious and open mind, being well read, keeping well informed, engaging in hobbies and meeting new people will help foster creativity. This will assist you in devising innovative methods and solutions, both as an investigative professional and in life.

Chapter 12

Integrity

Susan Pickman

According to Merriam-Webster, integrity is a "firm adherence to a code of especially moral or artistic values." In private investigation, that code is considerably more moral than artistic—it has to do with a combination of loyalty and honesty. Integrity forces an investigator to combine steadfast dedication to their client with an unwavering search for the truth, no matter what that truth might mean for the client, so long as the information requested by the client is able to be obtained legally. It also requires the investigator to work within the limits of the law and, ultimately, to avoid any actions that would cause them to cringe with shame when they look in the mirror. In other words, integrity requires ethics.

> Ethics are when responsible community members take the needs and desires of other people into account when they make decisions. They recognize that virtually everybody shares the "core values" of life, happiness, and the ability to accomplish goals. People who respect only their own needs and desires are taking the selfish point of view. Moving to the "ethical point of view" requires a decision that other people and their core values are also worthy of respect.
>
> *(Moor, 2004, p. 100)*

The commitment to act ethically and exercise integrity is one of the most important characteristics an investigator can have. The ability to retain contacts who can provide information and leads, acquire information legally, and then testify in court under oath is the hallmark of a top investigator. Those who demonstrate integrity can, and likely will, enjoy a long, honorable, and profitable career. If an investigator violates the principle of integrity, however, their ability to maintain a prosperous, high-quality professional life and a good reputation—plus, perhaps also the ability to sleep at night—will be substantially diminished.

In my personal and professional life, I have always inherently possessed integrity. Yet I suspect this may be due to the fact that I grew up in an environment where "doing the right thing" meant a great deal. My parents were the children of immigrants who came to the United States to avoid unduly oppressive and discriminatory governments. In the neighborhoods and communities where they lived, their word was their bond. I believe that they lived good lives through hard work and principled collaboration with their neighbors and friends. My father was an attorney and Officer of the Court, and my mother worked to integrate the school where we lived and to build a public library. She also worked for women's rights. These were all examples that made me into the person I am today: someone who adheres to ethical principles and strives to set the same example. To that end, I find it important to surround myself with others who demonstrate integrity and can help steer me toward the morally correct choice when complex circumstances arise and issues of right and wrong seem murky.

Ultimately, I am not sure whether one can be "born" with integrity; I suspect it has a lot to do with a person's environment. The good news is that an investigator can cultivate his or her own environment and intentionally choose the company of others who demonstrate integrity. Life choices are not as clear-cut as we imagine when we are young—therefore, the people with whom we surround ourselves have a significant impact on the choices we make. However, as the following case studies indicate, the most moral or ethical choices in a given situation do not always have obvious signposts.

Case Studies

Case 1

In one instance, early in my career, someone propositioned me to "flip" my loyalty from an existing client, who had already retained my services, to them. One day, I was approached by a friend whose parents were divorcing—let's call her Zane. Zane told me that her father, a successful professional of considerable means, was divorcing her mother, who had substantially less social and economic capital. Zane was afraid that her father, who knew all the judges around, would vastly overpower any protection that her mother might have in the divorce proceedings. Therefore, she wanted me to take on her mother as a client.

A few weeks after Zane's mother and I signed a letter of engagement, her father called and asked if I would have a cup of coffee with him at a local coffee shop. I said that I would, and we met. After the preliminaries of discussing mutual friends and associates, he pulled out his checkbook and said, "Whatever my wife is paying you, I will pay you double." I was shocked, but said, "What sort of a person do you think I am"? Then I stood up and left the coffee shop (but not without leaving money on the table for my part of the bill). The bottom line is that I could have made an additional $5000 just to start this investigation, but the transaction would have absolutely violated my principle of integrity. That would have been a nice sum of money to have, but it would have meant reneging on my loyalty to my initial client, Zane's mother, and essentially accepting a bribe.

The upshot of the case was that Zane's father was hiding many assets from both his wife and the IRS. Ultimately, I was able to provide the leverage that Zane's mother needed to live a decent life after the divorce, and I kept my integrity intact.

Takeaway: your word and your reputation should never be "for sale" to the highest bidder. Integrity often comes down to a choice between what is right and what is most profitable.

Case 2

In another instance, I was asked to give an expert opinion in a case that I didn't know anything about. By way of background, I am a court qualified expert witness in matters of Excessive Use of Force in Police and Corrections cases. A plaintiff attorney—let's call him Bill—once asked me how much I would charge to simply sign an affidavit in a Personal Injury case that he had written. The case involved a police officer who allegedly "roughed up" an arrestee on the way to the booking office. Bill said that his client had been severely injured after a fight with the police officer and it was clear that the police officer was at fault.

Since I worked as a police officer before becoming a private investigator, I knew what to ask in a case such as this. I asked if a private investigator had been retained to review the existing evidence and collect more evidence regarding the injuries to the plaintiff and any injuries to the police officer. I also asked if there were any surveillance videos of the incident and if they had obtained any videos from the booking office to determine if the injury had happened at the hands of the police officer or at the hands of a corrections officer or an inmate at the jail. Bill responded that they had not conducted any due diligence investigations but that they had photos of the plaintiff's injuries and the police report, so it was clear that the police officer had caused the injuries.

Without evidence, I was unable to make a proper determination. I challenged Bill's ethics by asking what type of expert witness he thought I was, and then I hung up the phone. Needless to say, in the absence of an objective investigation or additional factors, it would not have been appropriate for me to take the case, let alone later testify to the accuracy of the report that Bill had prepared and wanted me to sign.

Takeaway: a quick buck is not worth the value of your reputation or your personal integrity. Oftentimes it is better to pass on situations that appear unethical from the start.

Case 3

In yet another case, I was asked to embellish a report to favor a client. Generally, when I have a case that involves a plaintiff with injuries allegedly caused by a police officer, I insist on a two-stage engagement. First I review documents, videos, interviews, and other evidence in the case. If I believe that the client has a case that I can support, I move to the second stage when I write an affidavit or testify on behalf of the client.

In one personal injury case where I was working for an attorney's office—we'll call them Legal Lawyers LLC—police were alleged to have severely injured my attorney-client's plaintiff. When I reached the end of my fact-finding stage, I was convinced that the police officers did injure the plaintiff during the course of an altercation. However, facts indicated that the plaintiff was very much responsible, because he had attacked the officers with a dangerous weapon and was high on drugs and alcohol at the time. To complicate matters further, the circumstances that put the officers and the plaintiff in that situation were caused by negligence on the part of the dispatcher, who gave the officers incorrect information.

Legal Lawyers asked me to change my findings to make their case stronger by indicating that the officers were unjust in using serious force; this way, they could leverage a better settlement. I refused, and said they had to use my affidavit as written. Then, to make matters worse, Legal Lawyers still owed me a substantial amount of money and tried to shortchange me when they got less money for the defendant. I had to get my own attorney involved and only received my full fee after several months of wrangling.

Takeaway: sometimes the price of upholding one's integrity can be both fiscally and emotionally challenging. I also learned the value of getting paid up front!

Case 4

Prior to becoming a police officer, I worked for an employer whose system-wide practices fostered a climate of fraud. Fraud, by any other name, is stealing. In this particular case, I learned that having an education and being in a position to know better did not always ensure ethical practices.

In this particular role, I worked for a small mid-western university, which put me in charge of several million dollars. I had been asked to review fiscal practices and attempt to identify any indications of fraud. As I investigated, I quickly learned that a number of well-entrenched and fraudulent schemes were in place. Some employees would alter receipts to get more reimbursement. Others would alter time records to show that they were present and working when they really were not. In some cases, the supervisors of those individuals excused it by saying that the people involved didn't earn enough money as part of their salaries. However, there are no excuses for fraud. These were thieves. They may not have been willing to rob somebody at gunpoint, but they were certainly willing to ignore compliance and to steal.

The thieves held entrenched positions in this organization. In fact, before I arrived at my university post, it was filled by an embezzler, before the university fired him and replaced him with an honest person, who I replaced. Nonetheless, there were substantial disallowances from misusing funding. I could have gone along with everything the way it was set up, which was conducive to fraud. However, I knew that was not an option. Professional integrity is not only reactive—making a choice when a dilemma presents itself—it must be proactive, as well. To me, this meant setting up systems in such a way that those with malicious intent could not take advantage of the organization.

In the end, some of my recommendations for change and for establishing an honest and ethical environment were ignored. Unfortunately, this can happen, despite best efforts. Since my own sense of integrity would not allow me to tolerate such practices and I saw little hope of changing the corrupt nature of those around me, I kept my employment there brief. I was disappointed at my inability to change this system.

Takeaway: sometimes, no matter how hard you try, you realize you are swimming against the current. While persistence and dogged determination are important factors in improving an unethical environment, you must know when you have done the most good you can do and it's time to move on.

Case 5

In one case, I demonstrated my commitment to integrity by digging deeper into an investigation. At this time, I was in charge of internal affairs for local government. I was called to the scene of an arrest by my colleagues in the police department. They had discovered that an individual who was working for a contractor hired by the county—let's call her Tina—was embezzling funds.

The embezzlement was relatively straightforward, so that could have been the end of the case. However, as a Certified Fraud Examiner, I knew that by the time a fraudster is arrested for a specific crime, they have generally committed other frauds. Consequently, I reviewed Tina's prior job history and, by requesting an independent audit, was able to determine that she had committed a similar embezzlement at a previous organization.

Based on the audit, we were also able to uncover embezzlement had been occurring at a previous agency where Tina had been contracted. In effect, while on the face of it, the purpose of the investigation was to determine who conducted the fraud within a department, integrity demanded that we make certain that those violations had not happened previously and could not happen again.

Takeaway: there is no excuse for a lack of thoroughness in any type of investigation. The quick and simple approach may be easier, but it will almost never be a sufficient substitute for the patient and thorough approach. Thoroughness is always "the right thing to do."

Case 6

In another case, I exercised my personal integrity by furthering an investigation against a fellow employee. It is always a challenge when there is a fraud committed by one of your own. Although this had happened to me in the past, this time it happened in a law enforcement agency. There, we found an employee—we'll call her Sarah—committing theft. She was arrested, and that could have been the end of the case. However, something did not seem right in the way Sarah conducted herself. Specifically, she was quick to indicate that she was a first-time offender. This made me suspicious of her history, and I felt the need to investigate further. This presented a moral dilemma, because if I found something, she would potentially get into worse trouble. However, I decided to follow my instincts and pursued the difficult task of investigating a case that went against the interests of a colleague.

Upon investigation, I learned what happened. Through a series of phone calls, I determined that she had thrown herself on the mercy of the court as a first-time offender in a previous case, as well. She did not complete her restitution agreement, which required her to commit certain actions to make restitutions following her crimes and avoid further prosecution. However, this was never uncovered, as the prior investigator and the judge had retired. As a result, she was able to get away with her second "first-time offender" request. In effect, she was committing fraud.

When all of this came to light, she was unable to plead with the judge. Ultimately, we were not only able to stop her from committing fraud in our agency, but we established that she would have a criminal record in the future to warn off other entities.

Takeaway: more often than not, people involved in theft or fraud have been doing it prior to the incident that is uncovered. It is always worth a deeper look at criminal, civil, and judicial records and history—even if you have a personal connection to the accused.

Case 7

In another employee theft case, I had to perform the difficult task of informing a client that one of their most valued and trusted employees was guilty. This all happened when I was engaged to conduct a private investigation for an insurance company. The insurance company was insuring an organization—we'll call it Stuff Store—against employee theft and wanted to know if they, the insurance company, should pay a Stuff Store employee's indemnity bond following a fraud. Indemnity bonds reimburse the holder (in this case, Stuff Store) for fraud loss. The insurance company found that a Stuff Store employee had stolen funds totaling well in excess of the $50,000 bond.

Over the course of my investigation and that of the police, we found that the employee had used the stolen money to purchase an apartment. Furthermore, we learned this employee was a repeat offender. Stuff Store had no idea. While this finding was uncomfortable and difficult to divulge, we felt it was our duty to inform both the insurance company and Stuff Store.

We also achieved additional results for our client, the insurance company, as well as Stuff Store, by continuing our research. Although we could have stopped working due to our arrangement, our integrity and commitment to our client inspired us to persevere. In this case, both the insurance company and Stuff Store were most grateful, because we discovered an ongoing crime perpetuated by another Stuff Store employee. He was a longtime, trusted employee who was stealing from the company through a "ghost invoicing" scheme. Ghost invoicing is when fake invoices are created for goods or services that were never delivered. This employee had "hired" contract workers (who did not exist) to do "work" for the company (that was never performed), and then invoiced for that work using his own address as the "payable to" address.

Takeaway: generally, senior supervisors and managers don't like to hear bad news about long-term or high-performing employees. When briefing them on such results, it is important to carefully lay out irrefutable details or evidence that makes the wrongdoing you have discovered clear and will preclude any inclination to misinterpret or ignore your findings.

Case 8

In another instance, I exercised my integrity by saving a client money on his investigative bill. I was asked to look into a tenant—we'll name him Zahir—in a luxury sublet apartment. The client wanted to know why Zahir, who had paid the first and last month's rent to move in, now, six months later, had yet to pay a single month of rent. However, my client did not want to disturb his tenant, who he still thought would pay him. He felt that Zahir was so well heeled that his potential inability to pay was not an issue. My client believed Zahir must have simply forgotten to pay.

Why did he think this? Because of Zahir's résumé, which was very impressive. However, that was the only information my client had about Zahir. He had not required the man to provide any financial information or proof of employment. His reasoning was that he had met Zahir at a high-end social occasion and thus didn't doubt his credentials.

I did a background check on Zahir and attempted to verify the information on the résumé. Zahir's résumé showed that he had a PhD from a prestigious university. Universities do not graduate many PhDs, so I knew this would be easy to quickly verify. When I called the department at the university where Zahir allegedly got his degree, they did recall a similar student. However, there were critical differences. They said his middle initial was different, and the graduate in question was working on the West Coast and not in New York, where Zahir was living.

After that, I decided to check Zahir's address history. It turned out that one of his past addresses was that of a federal prison. I also checked on arrest warrants, of which he had several, for bad checks and fraud. That was evidence enough to show my client that his tenant was not the person he claimed to be.

In this case, my client had given me a substantial retainer, but I had not needed much time to get to the bottom of this case. I notified the client and returned a portion of the retainer because, based on my hourly rate, I had not used all of the retainer. In this instance, I could have continued on until I used up all of the retainer, but integrity dictates that you are honest about how you use your time. It is appropriate to set a rate that is commensurate with your knowledge, skills, abilities, training, and location, but you have an obligation to yourself and your clients to charge according to the time that you spend on their case—no more, and no less.

Takeaway: while it may be easy to justify to oneself that any offered payment "was earned," inside we know whether that is true or not. Fiscal fairness, to yourself and others, is an important part of your overall integrity.

Advice to Future Investigators

Integrity may be innate, but it is also significantly influenced by those with whom you surround yourself. As such, choose your company, both personal and professional, wisely. The types of moral choices people closest to you make will have an effect, overt or otherwise, on the types of choices you make. Therefore, your integrity depends upon surrounding yourself with loyal, trustworthy people.

In terms of more career-oriented advice, there are a few pitfalls to watch out for when preserving your integrity. First, do not "overestimate" billing time. Because investigators charge by the hour and their clients are unlikely to ever see the underlying work that has been done, it may be tempting to charge clients for extra time when work was not actually being done. However, both personal and professional integrity require that the number of hours worked and billed correspond directly with what has actually been done.

Second, respect the integrity of the investigation. Part of maintaining integrity is determining what needs to be done and how to go about accomplishing it. Sometimes this appears clear from the outset, sometimes not. Regardless of whether you need to revise your plan of action during the investigation, it is imperative to maintain professional standards—that is, an ethical code of conduct—throughout.

Finally, when you determine where your investigation needs to go (within the scope of your engagement), don't stop until you get there. Don't take shortcuts. Don't defer to the "easy road" if it will not get you the answers you need. And don't compromise your ethical and professional standards for the sake of making someone else "happy" or earning money unjustly. The integrity of a private investigator depends on seeing things through on behalf of clients, no matter how difficult or time-consuming. They are depending on you as the expert. Do not deceive them.

Reference

Moor, James H. (2004). Reason, relativity, and responsibility in computer ethics. In Richard A. Spinello and Herman T. Tavani (eds.), *Readings in Cyberethics* (pp. 40–54). Sudbury, MA: Bartlett.

Chapter 13

Professionalism

Bill Jorgenson

The Quiet Professional

"He's a real pro," "She did a really professional job on that project," "You handled that like a true professional." Words of praise? You bet. We all want to hear that about our good work, right? Of course. But what does the word "professional" mean? Why do we care? In this day of artificial intelligence, gossipy news and crazy politicians, does that word even mean anything anymore?

It certainly does. I would say now more than ever.

> The word "profession" comes from Middle English, from *profes*,
> adjective, having professed one's vows, from Anglo-French, from Late
> Latin *professus*, from Latin, past participle of *profitēri* to profess, confess,
> from pro- before + *fatēri* to acknowledge; in other senses, from Latin
> *professus*, past participle.[1]

Essentially, workers and tradesmen "professed" their skill and guaranteed that they would do a good job.

Being a professional applies to any and all forms of work. Professionals are true to their word and do what they promise. In fact, the navy SEALs have often been referred to as the "quiet professionals".[2] They have a strict code of silence and do not brag about their missions. As professionals, they are people who get the job done, often with great sacrifice, and without public praise. Doctors are another example of people in this category. So are investigators.

The Importance of Being a Professional in Investigations

In investigations, professionality is critical. In any trade, craft, or "profession," being known as a professional is the key to success. A professional person has mastered their field, and their reputation is based upon that mastery. It is challenging to beat a professional at their own game. This is true of any field. For instance, during a home remodeling project, I had a professional contractor come to my house to do the spackling on the walls I had put up. Why didn't I do it myself? I knew that I would need someone who knew what he was doing. Could I have done the job myself? Sure. Could I have done anywhere near as good a job as he did? Absolutely not. This is also true for investigations.

A professional investigator is known to be the absolute best in the business. If you break down the tasks of an investigator, they seem easy to replicate. Most of us have the ability to sit down with someone, ask a few questions and get some answers. However, a professional investigator can get at the truth when the person you are speaking to is hiding something. This quality separates a professional investigator from people who have a simple conversation with someone.

Professional investigators are highly skilled and know how to get results for their clients. These investigators build a rapport with their subjects, and get information in myriad ways, from direct questions to analyzing body language. And while some of us are just better at it than others, good interview technique is a craft, which the best investigators spend a career improving and refining. The same goes for many other investigative techniques, such as undercover work, surveillance, or data analysis. A true professional will always be looking for better ways to do the job. People with that attitude are highly sought-after individuals in their field.

Professionals have a positive attitude about what they do. They don't watch the clock. They work until the work is done, however long that takes. They don't complain and they don't put the blame on others when they come up short. A true professional admits to a mistake and moves on. After all, we have work to do!

If you are a real professional, you are flexible. You don't mind taking work home from time to time. You don't mind that call from someone needing help or that email from the office. That being said, most things can wait until the morning and people who know their business know when to ring the alarm bell and, more importantly, when not to.

The pros also don't take things personally. One big mistake I have seen amongst young assistant district attorneys is that they let emotions get in the way of their work. I've made that mistake myself. I have seen cases where the defense attorney makes a strong argument in court, and they get mad at the attorney. That's a huge waste of energy because the defense attorney is just doing their job. There is nothing personal. It's just business. Unless of course, the defense attorney is a hot-head as well. Then we would have all kinds of fireworks in the court room and not a lot to show for it—except maybe an annoyed judge and jury.

True professionals keep their emotions in check. Someone with a professional attitude about what they do is not going to let their mood, or their personal feelings, affect the job. Have there been times when I wanted to curl up and die in the courtroom when something bad happened? Of course. Were there occasions when I dragged myself in after a late night or I was upset about a fight I had? Sure. But I never let it interfere with what I was working on. In fact, I prided myself on not letting anyone see me sweat. Once I was in court, it was show time, and I had an audience. I knew I had to suck it up and get to work. Especially when I was in front of a judge who liked to give young lawyers a hard time.

Another habit of truly successful professionals is updating their team. They make sure everyone they work with is updated as to the current issues, understands their goal, and how the team is progressing towards that goal. Sometimes this is the hardest task. People can be hard to communicate with. Your colleagues may be unavailable, busy, or just not communicative. A true professional will take this into account. The best investigators brief their colleagues before an operation and make sure that everyone knows their job.

Second Class Boy Scout to Associate Commissioner

I never thought I wanted to be a lawyer. I knew I wanted to go to college, and everyone in my heavily academic family assumed I would become a teacher. After all, my father was a teacher. I was often told that I liked to argue, so I decided to go to law school. Of course, I had no idea what I would do with an advanced (and expensive) degree, but I knew I needed something more—just what that would be I had no idea.

The one class that I really enjoyed in my first year was criminal law. Admittedly, I wasn't very good at it, but I loved what it was about. It wasn't about what was within the four corners of the contract, or escheats at law (whatever those were) or making some banking corporation more money. Rather, Criminal law was about people. More importantly, what people did with the money they stole, the cocaine they smuggled, or the body of the poor person they just killed. Of course, being the only person on either side of my family who even attempted law school, I had no idea how to get into the field. I honestly thought at one point I would go back to that elevator operator job I had the summer after I graduated from college.

My interest in criminal law was confirmed once I landed an internship in the Staten Island District Attorney's office. Once I was in, I was hooked. Here were attorneys who went to court, argued cases, and put bad people in jail. They worked hard, they were enthusiastic about what they did, and maybe a little crazy. And there wasn't an escheat at law in sight. Most importantly, what they did mattered.

I became an assistant district attorney in the Richmond County (Staten Island) DAs office. In the beginning, like most rookie ADAs, all I handled were misdemeanor cases and new arrests. We weren't allowed near the felonies until we gained more experience. After a few years I was assigned to the office of the Special Narcotics Prosecutor for the City of New York where I started handling felony narcotics cases. It definitely felt like the big-time for me. After two years, I was transferred back to Staten Island, where I spent the bulk of my time prosecuting more drug cases and the occasional homicide.

Later, I took a job at the New York State Attorney General's office where I worked in the Criminal Prosecutions Unit investigating auto insurance fraud schemes. It was a small division, but we handled a lot of cases that a traditional DA's office couldn't or wouldn't because of jurisdictional issues, limited capacity, or expertise. Next, I found a place in the Nassau County District Attorney's office where I worked on fraud and public corruption cases. After that, I left prosecutions behind and joined the New York City Department of Investigation, overseeing investigations into fraud, waste and corruption throughout New York City. I also worked on training, outreach and a number of other matters within the agency.

Learning Things the Hard Way, or Don't Trust the Rookie with Anything Important

Over the years, I learned the importance of keeping a notepad next to my bed. Like any young assistant district attorney, I had a boatload of cases that I needed to keep track of. After a while, as the work kept piling up, I noticed that I was forgetting certain tasks. We all do that from time to time, but when you forget things in criminal court, bad things happen—drugs don't get tested, witnesses don't get notified that they have to come to court, and bad people go free.

Ever since working in Criminal Court, I have kept a notepad on my nightstand. I've often found myself waking up in the middle of the night remembering the work tasks I had to do. I would remember that I had to send the gun to the ballistics lab to make sure is was operable (if the gun doesn't work, it reduces the charge), or that I had to schedule an interview, or that I had to prepare for a grand jury presentation. I started to take work home with me, even if it was just in my head. Work became something more than tasks accomplished in a 9 to 5 timeslot. Doing what it takes to get the job done, including waking up at night just to check on something, became routine. Understanding that your day is not circumscribed by the clock is what makes for a professional attitude. That is what, bit by bit, I was learning. I realized that this is what being a successful attorney meant. I would have to work weekends, nights, and vacations, if that's what was needed to get the work done.

When Being a Professional Made the Difference

I have a lot of great examples to share about the great professionals I have encountered over the course of my career. The first involves my former colleague, John. His story starts with one random day, when my supervisor called me into his office. Before he spoke, I already knew what he wanted to talk to me about. Two of our colleagues were starting a trial in the Bronx. Jury selection was going on and the trial was finally getting underway. It wasn't the case of the century, but for our little unit, it was a big deal. A lot of resources and hours went into this investigation and prosecution and it looked like we were finally going to close the case. Unfortunately, the lead attorney had a sudden medical issue and could not finish the case. That left the second attorney, John, running this complex case all by himself on the eve of trial with no support. My boss asked me if I would go help him. Lucky for me I said yes. After a crazy couple of weeks involving long days in court, late nights, and weekends in the office, we got a conviction.

This case taught me a lot about how a professional conducts himself, especially in a tight situation. John never complained, never whined, never threw a fit. He worked hard, did the trial, and got the conviction. He was a pleasure to work with and never lost his cool. John was an experienced attorney who had just joined the office after several years in private practice. He had the attitude needed to accomplish the mission when everything was going wrong, and at the end of it all, he won the case.

Another person who exemplifies professionalism is my old supervisor, Tim. Tim is the "prosecutor's prosecutor." Anyone who has worked with him or seen him in action knows this—he sets the standard. Part of what makes Tim so successful is not just his dedication to the job, because a lot of people have dedication. Tim is courteous to everyone and keeps his cool no matter how bad things are going. I remember watching him in court when I was first getting started as a prosecutor. He could be in court on some terrible case, getting yelled at mercilessly by some bully of a judge, and his responses would always be in the same respectful tone. He made it clear where he stood without raising his voice or being baited by the judge. That isn't easy to do, especially when you're standing up in a packed courtroom on a major case receiving a lot of public attention. To have a judge shouting at you is humiliating. To Tim's credit, he would stand up to the judge in a professional manner, demonstrate why he was right and move on with whatever task he had to accomplish.

As a supervisor, Tim had a lot of responsibilities. One of them was making sure that I, as a junior ADA, was doing my job properly. If he needed to tell me to improve my job performance, he did so privately, quietly and firmly. Although I didn't like it at the time, I knew that in the end it was for my benefit, the good of the case and the good of the office.

Another true professional was my supervisor, Bob. I didn't work for him all that much, but what little I saw impressed me as well. Bob recognized that as the senior attorney in the office, he set the tone of the office, and people watched him closely. Any time you saw Bob, he had a smile on his face. We could be handling a major multi-million dollar fraud case with a whole host of challenging issues and he never let his stress show publicly. He made sure the case was handled properly with a minimum of fuss and without visible stress.

Bob's situation was unusual, in that he was a worker from the previous DA's administration. The tenure of the previous DA was quite long. Typically, any time a new administration takes over after a lengthy previous administration, there is a lot of turn over. Bob, who was a holdover from the previous DA's tenure, was unique because he survived such a challenging transition. I heard from many people how the new DA kept putting more and more responsibility on his shoulders while the new administration was taking shape. Yet, no matter how much piled up on his desk, Bob got the work done with a smile on his face. I had no doubt he was exhausted at the end of the day, but he would never show it.

Probably the most professional of all of my supervisors was Betteanne. I was fortunate enough to work with her in two different offices. The first was a district attorney's office where she was a bureau chief. In the second she was a senior level prosecutor, not a management position. In both roles she excelled. As a bureau chief, Betteanne had to supervise half a dozen young Assistant District Attorneys. Most of us were male, all of us were characters. Our bureau focused on narcotics cases, which were high volume, frequently litigated cases. This meant that we were in grand jury all the time, doing multiple trials a year and in court almost every day. We dealt with cops, informants and defense attorneys constantly. It was a high-stress, fast-paced atmosphere. On a good day, it was a lot of fun. On a bad day, you would rather be digging ditches in the rain. Betteanne ran the bureau with a great deal of patience and forbearance, and she kept us in line.

Betteanne rarely yelled; she didn't need to. She had earned our respect with the way she treated us. She made it clear she was there to make sure we had what we needed to do a better job. She didn't lose her cool. She didn't blame someone else when things went wrong, and, because of the high volume of cases, things often went wrong.

She was also an excellent motivator. Once, I had a disagreement with an undercover officer who did not come to court for a hearing, as planned. This caused me to be reprimanded by the judge and jeopardized my case. When the officer finally showed up, we got into a verbal argument. When I was finished yelling, Betteanne came to me and asked me what happened. After she saw how mad I was about how this person had screwed up our case, surprisingly, she told me to go next door, have lunch and a beer, and take the rest of the day off.

In this case, she was not rewarding me. She was motivating me. Betteanne paid enough attention to us as employees to know what we needed to motivate us. She knew that what I needed was a chance to cool down. At that moment, I was not in the right frame of mind to continue my work, and it would best for me and the office to take a break. She was right. Once I returned to work, I felt a lot better and I was able to be professional again.

We both joined a different office when the administration changed, and Betteanne was an incredible colleague. She was no longer a boss, but what we like to refer to as a "go-to" person. When a big case came into the office, it was given to Betteanne who functioned as the lead attorney. She delegated jobs and made sure we all knew what needed to be accomplished. She always had time to deal with our issues, and if she didn't know the answer, she knew how to get it.

In any business, an essential part of professionalism is your reliability. Can people rely on you when you say that you will be somewhere? Are you the person who follows up a promise with deeds and results?

I have a case which demonstrates a time when I overcame significant obstacles to fulfil my professional responsibilities. Once, when I was working for a large state law enforcement agency, I had been working on a lengthy investigation into corrections officers who were perpetrating a no-fault insurance scam. The leader of the group recruited other corrections officers and former inmates to assist him in his scheme. Essentially the fraud was as follows: two groups of individuals would rent two separate cars and then stage an accident. Each person in the plan would then seek out medical treatment for non-existent injuries. It took us a while, but we rounded up all the important players. One of them promised to give us intel on other matters involving criminal conspiracies. He looked like he would have good information, so following the defendant's arrest and the arrest of several of his co-conspirators, we agreed to work with him and conduct a preliminary debriefing.

Once the debriefing commenced, I learned he had several requests. Some we anticipated; the expected considerations for his cooperation, such as a chance at a reduced sentence. He also asked us to take care of one of the lesser players in the operation, "Joe". Joe was in his seventies and diabetic. He had played a small part as a passenger in one of the cars and was not looking at serious jail time, if any. He also didn't take care of his medical condition the way he should. Our informant, being a corrections officer, knew that if Joe went into the court system, he was most likely to spend several days in jail, while his medical condition was evaluated. During the debrief, it looked like we would work with the defendant, so I agreed that I would go to the court and recommend to the judge that Joe be let out without posting bail. We were taking a bit of a chance with him, but since Joe was a minor player, it wouldn't make sense to go too hard on him. In the meantime, it was an important gesture of good faith we could make to our new informant.

Then, the unexpected happened. A few minutes after I made my commitment to the defendant, as the debrief was moving onto its second hour, the lights suddenly went out. Our windowless conference room was plunged into darkness. Quickly, someone opened up the door to a darkened hallway. That's when we knew something was wrong. It soon became apparent to everyone in our meeting and on the floor, that the entire building was blacked out.

At this time, in New York City, this was a very scary situation. It was only two years after the 9/11 attacks and we were 22 stories up a building, without power, in downtown Manhattan. As more information came to us, we learned that not just our building, but the whole neighborhood was suddenly without power. No one knew what was happening at the time, but we all had the same thought—terrorism.

Yet, we had a job to do. I had promised the detectives who had custody of Joe that I would be in court to deal with this issue, so they wouldn't be stuck taking care of him indefinitely during the blackout. I had given my word to the defendant that I would honor his request to take care of his friend, and I had told my supervisor that I would handle the arraignment in court that day. I had given my word as a professional.

However, I was confronted with additional obstacles. Unfortunately, the court we were arraigning Joe in was across the East River in downtown Brooklyn, and traffic had come to a complete stop. The gridlock forbade cars from moving. In the days before Citi bike (New York City's bicycle sharing program), that meant one thing: I was going to have to walk to court. However, there was one bright spot in all of this. By the time we walked the 22 flights of stairs down to street level, we learned that it was an accident that had shut down the entire northeast power grid for millions of people. We were relieved to discover it wasn't terrorism.

We had another logistical challenge ahead of us. The walk from downtown Manhattan to downtown Brooklyn is 45 minutes to an hour over the Brooklyn Bridge. I had done it many times over the years and always enjoyed the experience. However, on the day of the blackout, this was not the case. As I walked up to the pedestrian footway, it was clear that this was not going to be a quick stroll over a historic scenic landmark. There was a major crowding issue. It seemed as though all of NYC was on this bridge. This was going to be a challenge. When the crowds reached the mid span over the East River, the already glacial pace of our walk came to a stop. I was running out of time, and I had to be in court. What was I going to do?

I realized I needed to innovate. I had noticed that the roadway, normally filled with cars, was fairly empty of vehicular traffic. Instead, hundreds of people were walking briskly along the road bed as cars and trucks slowly proceeded over the bridge. If I could get down there, I could get to court and do the arraignment before the court house closed down, without leaving Joe and my investigators stuck in the bureaucratic nightmare of a court system in the midst of a historic blackout. I also knew that there were catwalks that went from the walk-way, over the roadway, and which led to caged in ladders hanging down the side of the bridge. From there, a person could jump on to the roadway. "Just don't look down," I thought.

So that's what I did. I managed to get out over the roadway, throw my court bag on to the pavement, swing down the ladder and get to an area where I could make progress to court in time for the arraignment. At the end of the day, while a little worse for wear, I was able to deal with Joe's case and resolve the problem. My suit may have needed to go to the dry cleaners, but I kept my promise. That is what being a professional means.

When running an investigation, being a professional and having that reputation are often the difference between success and failure. When people recognize that you will do a professional job, no matter what the conditions, your word means a lot. When you make a representation regarding a problem or an issue, people will take you at your word, and trust you with a surprising amount of power.

I have a great example of this. It all started early one morning in Staten Island. Almost every district attorney's office requires that its assistants be on call, after hours, for a certain period of time. There are many terms for this duty, some offices call it "ride along" or being the "riding ADA". In Staten Island, we referred to it as "felony duty." In any event, the job is pretty much the same. An assistant DA is available to deal with any major crimes that occur over night. An ADA might be called upon to take a statement from a rapist, or write an emergency search warrant.

In Staten Island, in the 1990s, "felony duty" usually meant going to homicide scenes. ADAs were expected to do the following: take down the names and contact information of the detectives, witnesses, and any other important individuals, summarize the incident, and report back to the Chief Assistant District Attorney in the morning. I admit, these nights were long, but they could be exciting. They required the ADA to be "on their game" in the middle of the night, in bad neighborhoods, often in bad weather, and frequently with hostile or dangerous people. And, since we had to get there on our own, the travel was often a little scary. It was a challenge to remain professional in these circumstances. But if there was ever a time for professionalism, this was it.

On one particular evening, I received a call about a homicide that occurred in one of the housing developments on Staten Island. This was an area notorious for drugs and violence. It wasn't surprising to hear that a man had been killed in a playground in this area, shortly before midnight. By the time I got the call, I had only been asleep for a few hours. It was going to be a long night.

I reviewed the crime scene, spoke to the first officer on the scene, the crime scene investigators and detectives, and wrote up my report. Eventually, as the sun started to come up over New York Harbor, I made it back to my office. I reported what I learned to the Chief Assistant DA when he arrived at work. The homicide had started as a fight. There were signs the people involved had struggled for a while, and the victim was killed with a gunshot to the chest. I relayed all this information to my supervisors and went home early.

I forgot about the case, until a week or so later, when I heard that a man had surrendered to the police for his role in the homicide. Since I was familiar with the crime scene, I was asked to interview the suspect, along with the detective working the case. The suspect told a very involved story that initially didn't make sense. However, because I had been to the crime scene, I didn't immediately reject it, and advised my supervisor that it was worth checking out. This was where my reputation as someone who could be trusted to handle matters professionally, helped.

I contacted the defense attorney and asked him to do something very unusual. I asked him to waive the time limits on the investigation, so that I could get to the bottom of his client's admittedly bizarre story. Without divulging the details, the defendant's story was strange enough that even his defense attorney, Andy, had trouble believing it. I told Andy that if he consented to adjourn the case for a few weeks while his client was in jail, I would find out what happened. Because Andy considered me professional and a person of my word, he consented. Next, I spoke to the detective, Sue. Sue was an experienced detective and understood my thought process. We knew there were a lot of witnesses who didn't trust law enforcement and didn't want to come forward. This informed our strategy going forward.

Sue and I put the word out on the street—we just wanted to know what happened. We weren't looking to charge an innocent person, or someone who was defending themselves. Yet, a man had been killed, and we were going to find out what happened. Because of Sue's known professionalism when dealing with people who are skeptical of police, quite a few people actually came forward. The witnesses included prostitutes and gang members, drug dealers and homeless people. We treated every one of them with courtesy and respect. I am certain that the professional way we treated them was a big help in getting their cooperation. We interviewed them in my office, and had them testify in the grand jury, which was investigating the case.

The trust placed in me by my supervisors was also important in this case. As a result, they gave me tremendous latitude in how I presented the case to the grand jury. They knew that I would do a professional job of investigating this case. I was going to follow the facts wherever they led and do the job well, regardless of how anyone felt about the case, or the defendant.

Justice was ultimately served in this case. At the end of the investigation, we learned the truth was as crazy as it seemed. The defendant was indeed defending himself against the victim. We learned that the "victim" was on a number of controlled substances, had possessed two guns, one of which was never recovered, and was in a very agitated state when he confronted the defendant. Each person who testified in the grand jury corroborated a small piece of the defendant's version of the facts. Even the coroner's testimony supported the defendant's version of the facts. His testimony was unique, as Coroners almost never testify in the grand jury, yet we had him come in. The grand jury determined that the defendant had a legitimate right to defend himself and dismissed the charges against him. I attribute our success in this matter to our professionalism and dedication. We took the extra time to thoroughly investigate the case, and justice was served.

Don't be that Guy! The Price of Not being Professional

A good professional takes care of his/her reputation. Professionals mean what they say and keep their promises. I have an example of an attorney whose unprofessionalism cost him his reputation. Pete, one of my attorney colleagues in one DAs office, didn't seem to understand this. Pete had a terrible reputation for being untruthful— he would say that he had completed an assignment when he hadn't, he would show up late with a bad excuse, he would miss court dates and his colleagues would have to cover for him, etc. Simply put, he wasn't trustworthy.

One day, Pete was on trial. It wasn't a major case, just a typical street crime. The legal aid attorney made a routine allegation that he had not received all of the police paper work. As we know, this is a big deal. Prosecutors have to turn over every previously recorded statement—made by a witness regarding the subject matter of their testimony—before the witness takes the stand. The prosecutor is not allowed any surprises.

Pete was unprepared to defend a common legal claim, due to his lack of professionalism. In those days it was very common for defense attorneys to claim they had not received certain material, even when they had. Attorneys guilty of this practice would try to rattle the ADAs and get them to make mistakes. Experienced prosecutors and judges, however, were familiar with this tactic. The defense attorney's argument was usually defeated in a simple manner. The ADA would state on the record that he or she had turned over everything to the defense they were entitled to receive and give the court a list of documents submitted.

Unfortunately, in Pete's case, he did not submit a list. More importantly, when he said he turned over everything required to the defense, the judge did not believe him. This was very bad and very humiliating for Pete.

As a result, the court had to validate Pete's story. The court sent one of the court clerks and a court officer to Pete's office to look through his files. They were tasked with ensuring every document to which the defense was entitled, was actually turned over. Eventually, they validated that Pete had turned over all required material. However, his reputation never recovered. Eventually, he left the District Attorney's office. Pete learned the hard way that professionalism includes your reputation, and in this business, reputation is everything.

For a supervisor, professionalism is very important. Supervisors often have to deal with people they may not like, or have people do a job they know they could do better. Having the right attitude is what separates the good supervisors from the bad ones.

My friend had a supervisor who was quite unprofessional. This person did not listen, had no patience and jumped to conclusions without waiting to hear the facts. I remember sitting in on a meeting where this supervisor asked my colleague a series of questions, didn't give my colleague a chance to answer, and then yelled at him for failing to answer. It was humiliating and unprofessional. Needless to say, this supervisor failed to garner any respect amongst the people who worked for him.

Developing the Professional Approach

Finally, let me tell a story involving my own professional fumble. This was one of the worst days of my professional career. I was working on a murder trial. I was standing in a packed courtroom. This was a high-profile case. There were 12 jurors, the judge, the defense counsel, the defendant, and the victim's family. The press and several ADAs and interns were also watching.

My witness, a law enforcement officer, was testifying. Things were proceeding as they normally do. Then suddenly, the defendant's attorney told the judge he didn't receive the documents referenced by the officer, in advance of the trial. With this, he said "Judge, I move for a mistrial." This is the last thing you would want to hear, in my position.

In short, this would mean I would instantly lose the case due to procedural error. As discussed earlier, the defendant's counsel is entitled to all of the documents that will be used in the case. Here, the defense was entitled to the detective's scratch notes and anything else the detective may have written down about the case. Failure to produce this material is grounds for a dismissal.

The courtroom immediately went silent. All I could think, was "I'm going to lose this case. I'm really going to lose this homicide trial. The killer is going to get away with murder! All because I didn't ask the detective if he had given me all of his paperwork." My mind was racing. All I could think was that I should have double checked with the witness. I should have been on the ball. This murdering creep with the sleazy defense attorney[3] is going to get away with murder because I wasn't paying attention. More importantly, I know better. I should have spoken to the detective about anything I may have overlooked. I should have communicated with him better.

There were a lot of factors working against me in this case. This case evoked a lot of emotions for me. Although I knew to remain professional, it was hard to do so under these conditions. The homicide was particularly disturbing. I was overwhelmed with emotion and stress because of the terrible nature of this homicide. Additionally, the witnesses were a nightmare, the family was devastated, the case was all over the papers and my boss, my boss's boss and the DA were all watching me to see if I was able do the job.

Luckily, the case didn't end up in a mistrial. We turned over the notes, got the conviction and the defendant went to jail for a long time. Score one for the good guys!

What is the main takeaway of this story? Be a professional. Stay on top of your game. The job has to be your number one priority. You may have to deal with issues that disturb you, sometimes profoundly. You have to get past your own emotions and just focus on the task at hand. A professional will make sure that everyone working on a project is on the same page. A professional is confident enough to ask his colleagues for advice and help.

It is important to keep emotions out of your work as much as possible. We all have emotions, but learning to keep them under control and channeling them in a productive way is one of the most important things we can do. This is true professionalism.

Looking back, I realized that the single biggest mistake I made in that trial was allowing myself to become emotionally impacted by the case, to the extent that it affected my performance. As investigators and members of the law enforcement community, we regularly see and learn terrible things that most people never experience—the murder of a cabbie on his first night on the job, the knifepoint rapist who calmly and quietly tells you how he violated an innocent woman, the arson scene with multiple fatalities. In the end, we have to learn how to deal with the terrible stress that comes with this work. Failure to do so can lead to sleepless nights, bad decision making, and poor performance. In the worst cases, this can lead to substance abuse, mental illness and death. Make no mistake, the stress of this work can kill you if you let it.

By allowing myself to become too emotionally involved in the devastating impact this murder had on this man's family, I lost sight of what I needed to do. I needed to get a conviction and put the bad guy away. Instead, I let my emotions affect me to the extent that I was forgetting important details and forgetting those details could have cost me the case. At the end of the day, being a professional in the investigation business is about making sure the truth gets out ... whatever that may be.

Notes

1. Merriam-Webster dictionary.
2. Bonner, Kit (2002). *U.S. Navy Seals—The Quiet Professionals*. Atglen, PA: Schiffer Publishing.
3. The defense attorney later went to prison for his involvement in a mortgage fraud scheme.

Chapter 14

Ingenuity

Machiko Yamamoto

If you look up "ingenuity" in the dictionary, it will be explained as "cleverness", "originality", "inventiveness", etc. I believe that the qualities expressed by these words are very important for investigators. In this chapter, based on my experience, I will explain the "ingenuity" that is necessary for investigating any kind of crime, whether it is a common crime or a business crime.

First of all, let me start with my background. After graduating from a university in Japan, I went to the United States, where I received certifications in Crime and Intelligence Analysis and Crime Scene Investigation and got my master's degree in Criminal Justice. During my stay in the U.S., I worked as a volunteer at the Support Network for Battered Women and the Riverside County Sheriff's department Crime Analysis Unit. After that, I returned to Japan and worked as an assistant professor in a research and teaching position. Then, I worked for several years at a risk consulting company as a Security/Criminal Investigator. Now, I am a security manager at a leading global travel security assistance firm. I am also a certified fraud examiner (CFE) and a Certified Professional Criminal Investigator (CPCI). As a CFE, I have been very involved with the ACFE Japan chapter, conducting seminars and also creating original content for their newsletter.

My interest in criminology and criminal justice started when I was studying psychology and sociology at the university. There, I repeatedly heard that the number of atrocious crimes was on the rise. In the seminar classes I was taking at that time (social psychology and sociology of information and communication), I became quite interested in discovering the causes of atrocious crimes from a psychological and sociological viewpoint.

However, in Japan, research and educational institutions, including the university where I was enrolled, did not have criminal justice courses. The only way to receive a criminal justice education in Japan was at law enforcement agencies. All of that led me to continuing my education at a graduate school in the United States.

In graduate school, I was researching theories of crime and its causation and efforts for crime prevention at every level from individual to societal. I learned that crime was not easily defined or explained and that it originates on an individual level (biological and psychological perspectives), a societal level (the rule of law and deterrence theory) and also on both levels. For example, for a single instance of murder, the cause may originate in the personality and the characteristics of the person who did it, and, in some cases, there might be influences of alcohol or drugs. It may also be due to a grudge and from having been coaxed into committing a crime by others. For each of these factors you can also expand further. For example, when talking about personality, such causes as genetics, family environment, social interactions, early childhood experiences, and so on, can be named as influential factors. Overall, Criminology studies have been very interesting to me, connected me with a lot of colleagues and have in general been a meaningful experience.

My interest in criminology has shaped my personal definition of ingenuity. Like criminal justice, I think that "ingenuity" is created from existing academic knowledge. I think the same could be said for the other qualities discussed in this book. "Ingenuity" also includes the use of ideas and creativity. But what is needed for an investigation is not to create fantasy creatures nor to spin out fantastic stories, but to properly put together scientific components.

You probably know Thomas Alva Edison who was also known as the king of inventions. His inventions were born from his ingenuity. Although he had just entered elementary school, due to his excessive intellectual curiosity he kept asking his teachers many questions (they were series of "why" questions every time something was explained in class), so much that they even treated his behavior as abnormal. He had continued his observations out of strong personal interest so as to even cause accidents and was forced to leave his studies just three months after receiving a strong remonstrance from the school regarding his adverse influence on other students. It is said that his teacher told him at the time, "Your brain is rotten; You are crazy.", when parting with the boy.

Little Thomas Edison would end up proving them wrong. After that, he was taught by his mother who was a primary school teacher. She had conducted chemistry experiments using equipment and various chemicals she had gathered for him. She knew he was a very curious child, and this helped him accumulate his knowledge. It is said this is how he got absorbed into scientific experiments. Many of Edison's inventions related to electricity and telecommunications are based on the knowledge and methods of thinking cultivated through those experiments.

So, what is ingenuity? Ingenuity is emphasized in many fields such as ingenious planning, ingenious research and ingenious artworks, but many people usually think to themselves, "I am not a person who has any ingenuity." The more the people grow up, the more they realize about the dreadfulness of the course of their own lives as well as of their knowledge and experience, and through that realization they make conclusions about things being "impossible" for them. However, in most cases, there is no requirement for an ingenious person to achieve something "completely new to everyone," (a definition which has a tendency to stick to the word "ingenuity.") When one comes up with something "ingenious" like that, it may not be understood by anyone, and as in the case with Thomas Edison, people may view the person as strange or odd.

Rather, the type of "ingenuity" required for investigators is "a viewpoint which is different from that of the majority and the one that brings in a new value based on scientific knowledge and on general common sense." Thus in essence, ingenuity represents a "qualitative difference" that is present in their investigative work. So, what becomes the issue for investigators is how their knowledge is implemented.

Ingenuity is a skill that can help investigators work cases where the perpetrators are different from us. Incidents which are subject to investigation can involve people who are not immediately relatable to us. These people will not always think the same way as we do. Also, criminals and persons with deviant behavior are uncommon. When we think like that, we can understand how important "ingenuity" is for investigating various cases. People who cause incidents are not like ourselves, they are different people. What other people think often cannot be understood. In other words, "ingenuity" is required in order to approach such cases.

According to what my mother says, I am a natural investigator. From my childhood, my ability to assemble puzzles has been excellent. Also, it seems that my intuition was very sharp. I would always ask "why?" in relation to various things. I would be considering causes and reasons, such as why something had happened, and why it had happened, in relation to things in my daily life, and in the behavior of others.

In criminal investigative analysis, one learns the equation of "what + why = who" (a "person" can be narrowed down if an "incident/object" and the "reason/cause" are known). However, even though the criminals might be found by using this kind of thinking, the truth and reality cannot be revealed. That's when I noticed that by asking "why?" what I really wanted to know was not the "cause" or the "reason," but the "truth," the "facts," and the "reality."

I have had a habit for thinking this way until present day. I think by being naturally curious and having a habit of thinking deeply about the truth, it will be possible for me to even further cultivate my "ingenuity."

I would like to discuss the process I have used in my role as an investigator. As you will see, my investigative process is quite ingenious. In my work, I draw upon the disciplines of crime analysis, crime scene investigation, and forensic science. I also use fraud investigation techniques that I learned when I became a Certified Fraud Examiner (CFE).

The CFE is currently known as the qualification that indicates an expert on fraud. The CFE was created by Dr. Joseph T. Wells, an FBI investigator and later the founder of Association of Certified Fraud Examiners (ACFE). Wells defines fraud as "any crime which uses deception as its principal modus operandi." Wells designed the CFE for persons who conduct investigations and survey cases of fraud within organizations.

Per the founders of the CFE, both crime and fraud investigations require similar skills. Wells thought investigators needed the knowledge and techniques related to traditional investigations and surveys, along with the knowledge of accounting and business. As you can see from the origin of this CFE qualification, there is no difference in the qualities required of an "investigator" whether we speak of a street crime or a business crime. This training informed my investigative technique, which is multifaceted.

My technique is essentially a combination of multiple investigative techniques. Specifically, I employ crime analysis methodology, often used to solve street crime, to my fraud investigation cases.

In Japan, this technique is considered quite ingenious to the point where it is not widely understood. In fact, I am often met with challenges. Many investigators here have trouble combining these skill-sets.

I conduct many lectures in Japan on my technique of crime/fraud analysis. Attendees will often be challenged by my use of criminology and crime analysis to explain fraud-related crimes. One attendee at a recent lecture of mine said: "the importance of criminology is understood, but it's not possible to see how it can be used in practice". People here have trouble understanding how crime theories can be applied to practical business matters, such as in the case of preventing and detecting business crime. In other countries, such as the United States, I feel as though my techniques would be more acceptable.

The fusion of criminology with business in Japan is very difficult, and today it is still a challenge. Much of the knowledge gained from criminology and related academic studies is not related to business crimes or fraud. People in Japan don't believe that crime tools and techniques, which include DNA analysis and blood spatter analysis, are useful to business matters. In their limited view, that can be correct. But the value of criminology is understanding which techniques help to detect, prevent and deter fraud committed within companies—not how to capture violent criminals.

Although it is difficult for me to convey the value of my work, I use "ingenuity" when designing my lectures. And I focus on elements of my work that can be applied in practice.

For me, a huge amount of the knowledge and experience in investigations gained by me so far, has come from analyzing and studying the "substance" related to crimes already committed. Crime investigation skills help to illuminate that "substance," while the CFE certification adds the investigative skills related to obtaining evidence, reporting, testifying, and the prevention and deterrence of fraud.

The process of criminal investigative analysis is simple. It is as follows.

1. Collecting data, profiling input (victimology, forensic information, crime scene photos).
2. Decision making (a one-person crime, a group crime, victimology).

3. Crime analysis (organized, disorganized, mixed, disguised, etc.).
4. Creation of criminal profile, arrangement of apprehension.

To deconstruct a case, I often work backwards. My thought process in the investigative realm certainly demonstrates "ingenuity."

First, I think of "fraud" as a form of crime. In criminal investigation, the above process is repeated until the criminal's apprehension. However, in a "fraud" investigation, often times, it starts from a situation in which there is already a culprit (or a person who is thought to be the culprit).

How should such cases be dealt with? I consider the criminal investigative analysis process in reverse. In other words, I think about going back through the procedure from the situation in which the last step—"creation of criminal profile" and "arrangement of apprehension"—has been completed. Then I look to fill in the remaining three steps.

I analyze "fraud" using this "reverse" procedure. As a result, I gain an insight into the character, circumstances, the offender's background, and the corporate environment that led to the fraud being committed, and so forth. My aim is to use this information ultimately in furthering the traditional fraud examination tasks of obtaining evidence, reporting, testifying, and the prevention and deterrence of fraud.

I am very interested in the causes of crime in my country. I have conducted research on the "Japanese corporate culture of obedience and loyalty." To this end, I examined how a corporate culture is created, where employees follow the ideas of their managers and superiors at the company, regardless of the outcome. Some people can end up conducting illegal activities, due to their obedience and loyalty. I am interested in the reasons why people are obedient, in such cases, where the outcome is fraud.

I have found that, ultimately, clarifying the psychological, sociological and criminological factors involved in the process of employees engaging in illegal activities, that is, in the process of fraudsters becoming offenders, will lead to prevention and deterrence of fraud. In analyzing these factors, the method of reversing the criminal investigation analysis mentioned above has proved to be very effective.

Overall, criminal investigation analysis is very useful in fraud examinations. There are many parallels between crime and fraud investigations. One example is motivation, which is part of the fraud triangle (along with opportunity and justification).[1] The fraud triangle is a criminological framework for understanding business crime. I believe motivation is the most important part of the triangle.

This is how the concept intersects with general crime investigations. For some killers, they commit murder because they have lost control. For corporate fraudsters, many of them have also lost control. The "loss of control" for a fraudster can be demonstrated in their "motivation" for the crime. These motives, in a white-collar crime case, can include drug addiction or the pressure to "bend the rules" to meet quotas at work. In criminal investigations, the methods of analyzing criminals and victims and is also very useful for analyzing fraudsters, and their environments for committing fraud.

Overall, there is knowledge to be gained from studies on crimes, and applying this knowledge to research on fraud can also be considered as demonstrating "ingenuity."

Case Study

Now, let me introduce an example where ingenuity was used to solve a case. It is an example of a background check that I conducted.

The client, I will call it company A, which is the customer, found an article on the internet which talks about company B, who is their business partner, having a relationship with anti-social forces. "Anti-social forces" is an official government term that refers to organized crime groups and others with the potential for violence. In Japan, exclusion of anti-social forces has been promoted since 2007 and having transactions with anti-social forces constitutes a compliance violation.

Company A ordered an investigation on company B and its representative C. It is common practice for organizations such as company A to have as much background information as possible on the company and people they are doing business with. It is necessary for company A to take appropriate action if negative results are obtained.

Now I would like to provide more information about anti-social forces. Anti-social forces are an example of a unique way of thinking in Japan. Although they are similar to gangs, the Mafia, and so on, in other countries, the interpretation of this term is wider. Generally, it refers to the following kinds of groups or individuals.

- Military or similar organizations and their members conducting anti-social activities.
- Groups or individuals pursuing economic interests with the use of violence, power and fraudulent methods.

In Japan, the need to further strengthen efforts to cut ties with anti-social forces is being widely promoted. As anti-social forces further expand their power and scale with the profits they earn, the transactions which are the source of such profits are prohibited. Today, due to corporate ethics, many companies claim not to want anything to do with such anti-social forces such as criminal gangs. While various initiatives are being promoted, there is a lack of knowledge about criminal gangs. Such gangs can be sophisticated in their methods of acquiring funds. Thus, even in companies with a high level of awareness about excluding organized crime groups, there is a possibility they will carry out financial transactions with such groups as a result of not knowing they are involved with organized crime.

When investigating business partners and company representatives, one frequent problem experienced in background check research is the existence of companies with the same name and individuals with the same first and last names. This is challenging, because it can be difficult to determine which person or entity is your investigative subject. This happened with company B and representative C in this example.

There are many cases in which companies with the same name and persons with the same first and last names, exist separately. As a result, it is difficult for company A to determine whether the company B mentioned in a given internet article is the same company B that is their business partner.

In such a case, how should the target be identified? If there is information such as the company location, and information on dates of birth, etc., on individuals, this will represent clues for identification.

In Japan, police authorities have ready information on locations and members of anti-social forces, and when they are able to do identification, they can judge whether they are anti-social forces or not. In Japan, there are regulations regarding access to this information (Detective Business Act). General risk consulting companies are not authorized to access police data, but investigative companies, such as the one where I worked, can use a network that has access to police data.

However, in this case, the article was located but there was no information that could identify the location, and company A did not have information on representative Y, such as the date of birth, etc.

In order to judge whether company B and representative C belong to anti-social forces, we first decided to collect information on representative C. It is easy if the information can be obtained directly from the individual, but in terms of maintaining a good relationship, it is not desirable for it to be noticed that an investigation on having ties with anti-social forces is being carried out on business partners and related parties. In addition, if it is revealed that the company has ties with anti-social forces, it can lead to unfavorable or unexpected situations. The investigation needs to be kept secret.

We therefore used "ingenuity." First of all, the absolutely vital piece of information is the date of birth of the person who is the target. However, while this is helpful, there can still be challenges identifying the person, regardless of whether this investigation was conducted in Japan or the United States. There can be many people with the same birthday and with the same affiliation to organizations. However, in Japan, as opposed to the United States, if the date of birth and the affiliation of the target person are known, it is possible to order a survey from a network that can access the police data.

In the case of this client, however, they did not know the birth date. As you may know, the Japanese language has katakana and kanji notations and there is not much usage of the Latin alphabet. Therefore, if you know the kanji and the katakana and the workplace of the target person, you can identify the birth date using information from social networking sites (SNS), which in Japan refers to the top three most popular social media networks, which are Twitter, Facebook, and Instagram.

In this case, in order to obtain personal information on representative C, we gathered various pieces of information published on SNS, etc., and connected them all together.

Based on the information obtained this way, it was confirmed that the representative C was related to anti-social forces. After the survey report was submitted to company A, it stopped its transactions with company B, with this report as evidence.

How investigators can develop "ingenuity"

In order to develop ingenuity, it might be necessary to change your current way of thinking. I would like to introduce some Eastern philosophy and traditional Japanese practices that may help you to generate more "clever, original or inventive" thoughts—in other words, think like an investigator.

Investigative work never ends. For new investigators, this might seem overwhelming. Instead, it can be viewed as a process that will help to make you an expert investigator. In the process of gaining such expertise, you will naturally become more inventive in your way of thinking. As you become exposed to more people, techniques, and cases—engaging in tireless research—your creative thought processes will naturally expand.

The philosophy of the Japanese practice of "Dou" embodies this concept, finding that there is never an end to learning. According to Dou culture, as one's learning progresses, the person attains a higher level of mastery. There are several of the so-called "-do" as components of Eastern philosophy and the Japanese practices of "Dou" (cultural traditions)—e.g., as in 武士道 [bushido] (code of honor and morals developed by the Japanese samurai), 剣道 [kendo] (Japanese martial art), 柔道 [judo] (Japanese martial art), 茶道 [sado] (traditional tea drinking ceremony), etc.

As an investigator, learning the techniques of others can also help to expand your creativity. Eastern philosophy speaks to this concept. In Eastern philosophy, the tradition of learning from others can expand ones' creativity. Eastern philosophy speaks to the concept of wisdom, wherein learning tradition from others, then creatively expanding upon it, creates a new, informed tradition. Investigators can learn these techniques through educational materials, and mentors.

Chinese philosopher Confucius developed the "five constant virtues" (五常 五德). The "five elements" (五行 [wuxing] in Chinese) is a concept belonging to the natural philosophy that originated in ancient China. One of the five elements, called the "five constant virtues" (五常 五德), is necessary to represent the five qualities that surface when individuals living in groups are trying to achieve their purposes in life through letting their instincts show while, at the same time, trying not to harm the unity of their group. These are benevolence (仁), justice (義), courtesy

(礼), wisdom (智) and sincerity (信). Here, I would like to draw attention to "wisdom, 智".

The virtue of wisdom illustrates the value of experiential learning in sparking ingenuity. It has been said of this virtue that

> In order to learn, people need pioneers. Learning in one's own way becomes only one's own wisdom, but if you learn traditions from predecessors, you can create new things based on the traditions after having fully learned something. While following the traditions created by the predecessors, we add changes and conduct reforms on them, thus by repeating the process of learning and creation, we will increase the overall wisdom.[2]

A similar way of thinking exists in Japan's "do" practices and is expressed by "守破離 = Shu-ha-ri", which stands for "protect, detach and leave". This represents the three stages in mastering something. To clarify, they are the stages of: (1) learning fundamentals; (2) breaking with tradition; and (3) parting with traditional wisdom. These ideas also go along with "ingenuity."

In summary, originality and new perspectives are not born out of nothing. They are a result of chemical reactions that happen after acquiring a wide variety of ideas and perspectives.

Ultimately, the process of gaining "ingenuity" is similar to cooking. We use the various pieces of knowledge we have previously acquired as ingredients and make them into a sauce, a method for approaching the essence and truth of events.

"Ingenuity" is not what you can get right away by just doing something. It is, however, something that will be cultivated gradually if you never give up and always patiently keep the attitude of having new doubts and discovering new perspectives.

Notes

1. The author of this theory is criminologist Donald R. Cressey.
2. Source: www.jpc-net.jp/cisi/mailmag/m105_pa2.html.

Chapter 15

Empathy

James A. Gagliano

Empathy is an important quality for an investigator; however, it is one that may not come naturally in this profession. Law enforcement is a profession in which its practitioners have traditionally been conditioned to view feelings and emotions as avoidable weaknesses or vulnerabilities. Sworn peace officers have historically relied on the projection of strength, implacability, and a purposely impassive command presence to impel cooperation and compliance. This is achieved by the practice of repetitive, emotionless, mechanical training exercises that reinforce muscle memory and contribute to precious life-saving fluidity during in extremis encounters. "Action always defeats reaction," so the combat truism goes. Why waste valuable seconds processing the motivation and backstory of the potential threat in front of you? The immediate life and death implications are obvious. Or, as American writer Sherrilyn Kenyon famously put it: "Better to be judged by twelve than carried by six." A millisecond may determine a confrontation outcome with scant opportunity to exhibit empathy—the ability to understand, without necessarily sharing, the feelings of another.

Adoption of this survival mindset would make it appear that empathy is a luxury that the average investigator simply cannot afford. That thinking is outdated and wrongheaded. It also results in instances of over-policing, brutality, or mistreatment of the citizenry we are sworn to protect and serve. As we have experienced in incidents between 2014 and 2016, it can foster a simmering resentment that has boiled over into assassinations of police officers in New York City, Baton Rouge, LA, and Dallas.

Proven Solutions

I have successfully employed empathy as part of a comprehensive law enforcement strategy. In Newburgh, NY, I used empathy to transform a crime-ridden city into a safer place. My early efforts were recognized by journalist Patrick Radden Keefe in his September 2011 article, "Welcome to Newburgh, murder capital of New York: can FBI Agent James Gagliano make Newburgh safe?"

At the time, Newburgh was an impoverished city of 29,000 inhabitants that was rife with gang warfare, illegal drug peddling, hopelessness and despair. When I arrived in 2008, Newburgh was hemorrhaging. Assigned to oversee FBI operations in the region, I assembled a team and we attempted something radically different. Our tactics gained an undeniable measure of success. Newburgh has since rebounded, and according to numerous indicators, has made somewhat of a miraculous comeback,[1] with violent crime incidents[2] decreasing appreciably. This, from a city saddled with a vastly different headline "Obama hears of Newburgh violence."[3] only 18 months prior.

The transformation that started back in 2011 relied on three components, predicated on a pragmatic sensing of the "big picture." For those of us dispatched to grapple with the Newburgh crime problem—we had to care. Although we were provided with ample federal funding and had the full support of the United States Attorney's Office for the Southern District of New York, a satisfactory budget and federal laws would not have solved the crime problem. In his article, Keefe outlined part of the revolutionary strategy when he said:

> The "emergency transfusion of federal dollars was crucial, but, as Gagliano knew as well as anyone, rental cars and overtime payments would not be enough to stem the violence. To permanently restore order to Newburgh, he would need to take down the gang leadership today, but also to cut off the supply of fresh recruits who might run the streets tomorrow. Achieving that would require a tricky mix of blunt force and empathy—an unusually compassionate law-enforcement strategy, but one which Gagliano was well positioned to administer."[4]

The empathetic strategy was not initially embraced by the "safe streets task force" in Newburgh, comprised of cops, state troopers, and federal agents. It was, no doubt, a difficult sell to grizzled investigators and street cops. They had become numb to the violence and chafed at what they perceived as "going soft" on street thugs. But there was nothing "soft" about the strategy. It was designed to use federal racketeering statutes to hammer the worst of the worst of the gangbangers and narcotics traffickers. Yet it was also designed to stave off the flow of recruits that would presumably fill their ranks; giving the gang's potential replacements and recruits another option.

The strategy required community involvement. Therefore, some type of outreach effort had to be adopted and implemented. The solution was achieved through coordination with the local scholastic school system. I gave lectures to the local community on early intervention strategies and shrewdly leveraged my network of available mentors through the United States Military Academy, my alma mater, and the local Boys & Girls Club where I had volunteered as a basketball coach for years.[5]

My strategy also required funding. I was interested in establishing a local community center[6] to proactively reduce crime by actively engaging local young people. However, a challenge presented itself. As an employee of the federal government, I was not permitted to use my position to fundraise.

Thus, I adopted an "outside of the box" stratagem to raise money, resulting in exciting new community developments. This involved convincing a local businessman and motorcycle builder, Paul Teutel, Sr., of Orange County Choppers, to get involved. The collaboration[7] resulted in a bike-raffle that raised much needed funding or seed money. Again leveraging personal contacts I made in the region, I convinced a prominent local businessman to provide grant money to convert the abandoned National Guard Armory into a vibrant multi-purpose athletic/academic hub. This resulted in the Newburgh Armory Unity Center (NAUC), which has since become a model charitable project, the envy of the not-for-profit industry, and the crown jewel in Newburgh's resurgence as a community.

All of this speaks to the criticality of empathy, as applied in conjunction with the stark justice truism of choice–decision–consequence. The citizens of Newburgh never viewed me as an outsider or as a cold, impersonal, uncaring caretaker of the law. They viewed me as a partner and part of the solution. This highlights the value of empathy in law enforcement investigations.

Experience also matters. It is nearly impossible to identify a single profession whereby a practitioner's experience is not considered a value-added commodity. The law enforcement profession recognizes the value of those with insight into the best practices when working with the public. For the investigator, the ability to communicate effectively with witnesses, crime victims, criminal perpetrators, and civilians is essential. Effective communication begins with the interlocutor making every effort to place themselves into the shoes of the person to be engaged. In other words, every investigator, serving as a sworn, armed instrument of the state, must exhibit the requisite emotional maturity and empathy befitting such a powerful position, one where the appropriate use of force in escalating situations may be justifiable. Ultimately these consequential interactions may result in a split-second decision to take a life—a most sobering responsibility.

Investigations, formal inquiries or systematic studies of events or circumstances are a staple in the law enforcement realm. We pose questions in order to solicit answers that are intended to determine guilt or innocence. Exhaustive, probing, and intrinsic questioning is purposely designed to provide answers. It also disassembles preconceived notions or faulty hypotheses. In the course of law enforcement duties and functions, the hyper-scrutinization of evidence and available facts is conducted during the latter stages of an investigation. Responding investigators do not typically arrive at a crime scene in the capacity of a first responder. First responders often answer a call from a dispatcher, or encounter criminality during routine patrolling, arriving on scene in an information-vacuum. They are starved for facts, and forced to make immediate assessments and real-time judgments. This is the typical realm of the classic highway patrolman or beat cop. While investigators are often afforded the benefit of additional relevant facts, their interface with the public relies on the same essential tools we instill in our first responders.

Law enforcement often serves as an intermediary in disputes. When conflict resolution efforts fail between parties, violence and criminality may ensue. This leaves the investigator in the role of mediator between persons in order to attempt to reconcile differences and determine the guilt or innocence of those involved. In this response and assessment role, law enforcement personnel are often categorized as a third-party intermediary (TPI). When investigators are thrust into this role, the individuals they are likely to encounter, perpetrators, witnesses, and/or victims, are all in a heightened state of anxiety or stress. Therefore, their actions/reactions are less predictable and exponentially more dangerous to everyone involved, including themselves, responding law enforcement, and bystanders in close proximity to the scene. Therefore, the ability to understand and appreciate the motivations behind actions is critical.

One of the tools that FBI hostage negotiators in the field utilize to engage or interact with subjects is defined as active listening skills (ALS). Pre-eminent in dispute resolution circles, ALS is widely acknowledged to consist of six skills: paying attention, withholding judgment, reflecting, clarifying, summarizing, and sharing. This technique involves connecting with a subject, and requires empathy—not sympathy—to relate to a subject's circumstance, while not condoning the activity or conduct.

In this context, empathy is a fundamental leadership tool that law enforcement must consider when engaging with the public. For the distraught or conflicted criminal, witness, and victim, it is essential that law enforcement creates an environment where these incident actors believe that the investigator is truly interested in the conversation and is vested in the engagement's outcome. One of the most essential human needs is the feeling that one is understood. For investigators required to multi-task in dynamic, rapidly-evolving situations, they must take the necessary time to connect with the interviewee.

The ability of investigators to empathize with their subject facilitates crisis intervention. The FBI's Critical Incident Response Group (CIRG), where I was assigned during various points of my career, views crisis intervention as a critical skill-set for law enforcement. During critical incidents, which we may characterize as all criminal events, it might be difficult for investigators to think rationally. Intense emotional reactions proliferate and further complicate difficult circumstances. During this period of heightened tensions, the subject's perception of reality is what counts. If any participant feels they are in crisis—then a crisis exists. According to CIRG, while individuals are in this state, they can experience unpredictable cycling through alarm, anger, frustration, paranoia, betrayal, and fear. FBI hostage negotiators and frontline special agent investigators are taught to resolve the crisis by recognizing the onset of these emotions to assist the subject in returning to a functioning level of comportment. The awareness of symptoms and the emotional cycle is aided by the inherent empathy of those charged with interdicting crime, minimizing its impact, and providing aid to those affected/impacted by same.

Investigators can also use empathy to improve their case management skills. Investigators are leaders. Leading a conclusive investigative effort requires the deft employment of legal, coercive techniques to help uncover the truth. Investigators, as leaders, can exert influence in their casework by being perceived as exhibiting real empathy—caring about the circumstances in which a victim, witness, or perpetrator currently finds themselves.

Active listening skills can improve an investigator's ability to empathize with their subject. Effective listening can enable investigators to better gather insight into the motivations and concerns of the interview subject.[8] Recognizing that one of the most essential human needs, to be understood, is critical. In other words, the conveyance of true empathy can be a value-add in the investigative realm in the search for truth. This skill-set is a necessity, and not a luxury for the earnest investigator.

Discerning the motivations of our investigative subjects is key to understanding root causes and contributes to early detection and prevention. The more information we get from our subjects, the richer the investigation. However, our ability to extract information can prove challenging when we are faced with a subject whose actions might repulse us. Our natural inclination is to be revolted by the misconduct, mayhem, or unprovoked violence, wrought by a gangbanger, extremist member of a hate group, or radicalized terrorist. We must earnestly fight the urge to turn that revulsion into "fuel" for their hatred or perverted ideological bent. Despite adversity, we must be sure to remain steadfast in our ability to resolutely perform our job and obtain necessary information to inform our investigation.

Scholars have identified ways to handle these ethical dilemmas. In a *Psychology Today* article, titled "Empathy for terrorists, bullies and delinquents? How understanding helps make us all much safer," Michael Ungar recognized the investigative value in empathetically understanding the motivations of terrorists. For him, it is understanding how one alters behavior. This informs how law enforcement investigators should attempt to handle those predisposed to peddle terror or engage in criminality.

Ungar discusses how his experience informed his viewpoint. When reading about the 2012 al-Qaeda terrorist convictions in New York, he observed how the disaffected, disenfranchised, possibly brainwashed terror-merchants managed to evoke empathy, writing

> I can't help but feel a pang of empathy for men who come across like needy children in search of a friend, a father figure, or both. I don't say this to excuse what they did in any way. My motivation is instead to find the best way to change them, or prevent others from becoming just like them.[9]

Ungar further suggests we endeavor to understand and appreciate individual context as a derivation of violence. For him, "That act of looking for clues in the past to the actions of individuals in the present is one of the roots of empathy." This inquiry can help investigators to understand how violence fulfills the individual perpetrator. He suggests the following methods of inquiry, which are particularly useful to investigators, to arrive at the contextual information.

■ Get the full story. Understand the individual and where the individual grew up.
■ Consider the individual's actions in comparison with others who grew up facing the same challenges. Is the violence reasonable, or normal, under the circumstances?
■ Ask ourselves what alternatives were realistically available to the violent individual who grew up looking for connections, power, social status, and meaning. How else could they achieve these good things that unfortunately can be achieved through extreme violence?
■ Advocate for solutions that provide the next generation of potential terrorists, bullies and psychopaths with sources of support and self-expression that are just as powerful, and socially acceptable.[10]

Meanwhile, Ungar is clear that empathy is about understanding and not tolerance. He is unequivocal in his condemnation of same. Empathy does not equate to tolerance, as he suggests here:

> While I may extend terrorists, bullies and criminals empathy, that doesn't mean that I don't want to see them controlled, disciplined, and sometimes punished. I have a right to feel the way I do, especially if their behavior is dangerous to others. But to intervene in spite of my repulsion, that is a different thing altogether.

What follows is an excerpt from a published Q&A I participated in with world-renowned terrorism expert, Paul Cruickshank. It illustrates the work that I did while head of the FBI's Crisis Management and 24/7 Operations Center Programs in New York. My assignments included oversight of the SWAT Program, Crisis Negotiation, the Special Agent Bomb Technicians, and the Hazardous Materials Response Team. Here, you will see the value of conducting advance research on your subject that you can use to understand their motive. As you will see, this research is critical towards building empathy for the subject. In the excerpt that follows, I discuss the use of "speculative intelligence" to develop empathy when investigating a given subject when working in a hostage rescue capacity.

> In [one] case, we had several advantages as we knew who we were dealing with—the case squad had completed an exhaustive workup on the subjects—and we had time to painstakingly prepare in advance. We also had the warehouse wired up with audio and video feeds

because we had a solid cooperating witness. The CCTV video feed accurately showed us in real time where people were positioned and where weapons were emplaced in the room, so we were able to make the entry with informational superiority. Knowledge, or intelligence, is power and a force multiplier. In situations where you are responding to an active shooter or a hostage standoff, you have much less time to appraise a kinetic situation. In those instances, rehearsals, standard operating procedures, and experience are what you rely on to augment the momentum necessary to effect a successful rescue.

As a responding tactical unit, the success of your action is always going to depend on your evaluation of the situation before going in, reducing as many variables as conceivably possible. The key here is to obtain what we call "speculative intelligence"—a profile assessment, if you will—to figure out how likely it is the hostage-taker(s) are going to kill the hostage(s). You need to understand the mindset, desperation level, and motivation of the attacker(s). In all cases, you need to come up with a "hasty assault plan" basically right away. That then forms the genesis of your "deliberate assault plan" as intelligence improves and more resources are assembled.[11]

Advice to Future Investigators

The ability to communicate and to build rapport with the public is an essential attribute in order to achieve success in this field. This quality should spring from the mammalian system that is universally desirous of showing care and concern for "our own"—for humanity. Law enforcement must endeavor to treat and consider those we are sworn to protect and serve, as members of an extended human family. Viewing people as empty, nameless, faceless entities, or trifling annoyances during an otherwise peaceful assigned shift, makes it far more likely that misunderstandings, leading to unnecessary encounters, may occur.

When afforded an opportunity, take time to truly pay attention to the people with which you, as an investigator, interact. It goes beyond simple safety precautions, but speaks to who we are as a profession. Building relationships is essential to gaining trust. Without empathy, an investigator is unprepared and missing an important tool to aid in the successful completion of their investigation. Forever treat this valued characteristic as essential as the other inanimate objects associated with your trade. It will serve you well and may ultimately save a life—your own or someone else's.

Notes

1. Bellamy, Lana (2019). Newburgh's in bloom with new transplants from NYC area. *Times Herald-Record*, June 30, 2019.
2. Bellamy, Lana (2019). "Violent crime drops significantly in City of Newburgh." *Times Herald-Record*, May 9, 2019.
3. Murphy, Doyle (2010) "Obama hears of Newburgh violence." *Times Herald-Record*. March 6, 2010.
4. Keefe, Patrick Radden (2011). "Welcome to Newburgh, murder capital of New York: can FBI Agent James Gagliano MAKE Newburgh safe?" *New York Magazine*, September 23, 2011.
5. Murphy, Doyle (2010). "FBI briefs Newburgh on gangs." *Times Herald-Record*, April 15, 2010.
6. Murphy, Doyle (2010). "Center for hope: The antidote for violence." *Law Enforcement Bulletin*, November 5, 2010.
7. FBI New York Press Release (2010). "Orange County Choppers partners with the FBI and the Hudson Valley Chapter of InfraGard to build an FBI-themed Chopper." August 9, 2010.
8. Bradley, D. and J. Jancewicz (2016). "Focus on leadership: leading through listening," *Law Enforcement Bulletin*, March 9, 2016.
9. May 2, 2012.
10. Ungar, Michael (2012). "Empathy for terrorists, bullies and delinquents: how understanding helps make all of us much safer." *Psychology Today*, May 2, 2012.
11. Reprinted with permission from the author. Cruickshank, Paul (2017). "A view from the CT foxhole: James A. Gagliano, Former FBI Hostage Rescue Team Counterterrorist Operator." *CTC Sentinel*, 10(5).

Index

Printed in the United States
by Baker & Taylor Publisher Services

Printed in the United States
by Baker & Taylor Publisher Services